THE PINE CREEK RAIL-TRAIL GUIDEBOOK

A Bicycle Ride Through History

LINDA STAGER

Happy Trails...
Linda Stager

Address all queries to:
Linda Stager
PO Box 461
Wellsboro, PA 16901

Address additions and corrections to PCguidebook@gmail.com

All uncredited photographs were taken by the author. Trail maps are courtesy of Scott Adams Enterprises. Pictures are cited as necessary.
ISBN 978-0-9862539-7-3
First Edition

Published by Scott Adams Enterprises and Linda Stager

ACKNOWLEDGMENTS

I am grateful for several things that have made this book possible to share with you. I especially thank these authors for their inspiration for this book and encourage you to read their works:

Steven Owlett, "Seasons of the Tiadaghton, An Environmental History of the Pine Creek Gorge", 1993

Chuck Dillon, "Hikes in Pennsylvania's Grand Canyon", 2011

David Ira Kagan, "Pine Creek Villages", 2008

Dave Kagan, especially has been a good friend, mentor, editor, and person of knowledge who has been supportive of this work from the moment I told him of it. Dave knows the rail-trail perhaps better than anyone and logs around 5000 miles a year riding it. His information and photos are smattered throughout this book.

Furthermore, I send a shout out to Chuck Dillon whose hiking books have inspired people over the last 20 years and who has been supportive in allowing me to quote sections from his classic books.

A fond acknowledgment goes to the cyber community of the Pine Creek Rail-Trail Facebook page. I have spent many hours there enjoying the company and support of the people who frequent that page. There are many fine folks in that community who enjoy the rail-trail as I do and who champion it as a magical and soul-soothing place.

Thank you to those who have gone before us. The people who lived here, worked here, and built what we enjoy today as a rail-trail. To those who had the foresight and the ambition to successfully negotiate the deal that gave us the rail-trail, I say Kudos.

And a special thank you to the Pennsylvania Department of Conservation and Natural Resources (DCNR), the Pennsylvania Forestry Department, the Pennsylvania Game Commission, and the countless volunteers for their diligence to maintaining this natural resource in such a fantastic manner for us all.

INTRODUCTION

After retirement, my health took a turn for the better and with renewed abilities and energy, I set out to re-learn riding my bicycle. My goal was to enjoy nature in an easy-to-pedal setting. The Pine Creek Rail-Trail, one of the premier rail-trails in the Northeast, certainly met my criteria and was only three miles from my house.

With a little trepidation, I headed out on the trail but within hours, I knew I loved the physical activity and the environmental stimulation. It was simply beautiful there.

The Pine Creek Rail-Trail is a 62-mile long bicycle path, built along an unused historic railroad corridor. The path is well groomed and clean. It is constructed of fine-packed limestone gravel and slices its way through pristine farmlands, wilderness areas, and suburban neighborhoods. It is never difficult riding, with only a 2% grade over the entire path. Comfort stations (pit toilets) are spaced along the trail. It gives riders an up-front view of the Pine Creek Gorge, with a large creek known for its wild beauty and brief sections of rapids and riffles, its deep mature forests, clear mountain-fed streams, and seasonal waterfalls. The trail is mostly shaded and usually not crowded with visitors. Often a rider or walker is alone in nature for miles on end. Wildlife is often but a glimpse away.

Each season of the year offers its special view of an untainted, exquisite, natural wild area.

Rich in history and natural beauty, this is a ride through the timeless Pine Creek Valley, where the steps of Native Americans, miners, loggers, and families echo close by, just in another dimension, the dimension of time.

There are several Access and Parking areas spaced every 8 miles or so along the trail that allow for easy segment riding. Shuttle services are also available for those riders who want to ride one way and have their car available at the end of their ride. See Page

176 in the "What Do You Want to Know" section for details.

This Guidebook is divided into 7-13 mile sections of the rail-trail and narrates a bicycle tour of the old railroad corridor. You and I together, will ride along, with me pointing out things and telling stories of interest. There are two sets of mileages: a section mileage and overall mileage on the trail. We will ride North to South.

Get ready for a stretch of solitary, quiet communion with nature, except with a tour guide. Enjoy.

TABLE OF CONTENTS

PINE CREEK TRAIL

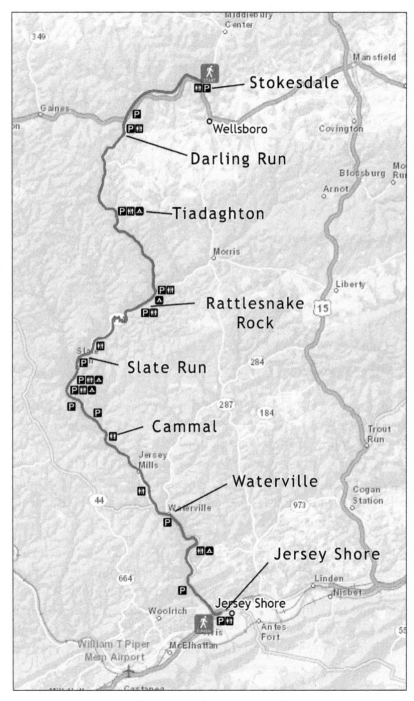

Stokesdale

Darling Run

Tiadaghton

Rattlesnake Rock

Slate Run

Cammal

Waterville

Jersey Shore

PARALLEL UNIVERSES: A TRIP THROUGH HISTORY

(THE STORY OF THE PINE CREEK RAIL-TRAIL PROJECT)

The Pine Creek Rail-Trail travels for 62 miles along the railroad beds of several former Pine Creek railroads. Eighteen miles of the trail follow the floor of the Pine Creek Gorge, also referred to as the Grand Canyon of Pennsylvania. On smooth crushed stone, the mostly level trail runs from Stokesdale Junction, outside of Wellsboro, PA to Jersey Shore, PA, through the historically rich and timeless Pine Creek Valley.

The railroad along Pine Creek opened in 1883 as the Jersey Shore, Pine Creek, and Buffalo Railway. It was built to transport timber to sawmills in the lower part of the Gorge. The Fall Brook Railroad took over in 1884 and the railroad carried coal north into New York State. By 1896, the railroad was carrying seven million tons of freight and three passenger trains ran daily along the exact locations on which we now ride.

Eventually, the New York Central Railroad took over the system and from 1914 until 1976 the locomotives sported the NYC logos.

Conrail took over the lines and ran trains through the Gorge until the last freight train passed through in October 1988.

Thus ended more than a century of service.

In July 1988, Conrail filed to abandon the rail line and the following month the Lycoming County Commissioners petitioned the state to give priority to using the abandoned right of way by only non-motorized vehicles. About the same time, the concept of the rail-to-trail was presented within the then Department of Environmental Resources.

By September of that year, an agreement had been worked out and interim trail usage was granted to the Rails-to-Trails Conservancy in return for Conrail's right to remove the tracks and facilities along the way.

Two years later, Pennsylvania's legislature passed Senate Bill 967 which allowed the state to purchase the railroad right of way for $1 and to initiate the trails we now know.

The construction of the first section of the trail—the nineteen mile Ansonia to Blackwell section—began in 1995 and opened the next year. In June 2001, another 23 miles, from Rattlesnake Rock to Waterville opened. The Waterville to Whitetail section opened in 2005 and the southern terminus at Jersey Shore was completed in 2006.

The final section, from Ansonia north to Stokesdale Junction was completed in 2007.

The Pine Creek Trail, nineteen years in the making was now rideable from end to end.

The Pine Creek Rail-Trail is enormously popular because of its stunning views and quiet serenity.

Miles of split rail fencing line the eight-foot paths and the road-beds are kept in superb shape for riding. The trail passes through what has been described as some of Pennsylvania's most imposing terrain. Yet, the trail terrain is relatively flat and visitors can tour in relative comfort. For 55 of its 62 miles, it parallels Pine Creek, providing breathtaking views of a deep mountainous gorge, numerous mountain runs, and potential wildlife sightings.

The trail passes through two state forests—the Tioga to the north and the Tiadaghton to the south. There are few commercial intrusions, except for limited stores and restaurants in towns along the way.

The trail is host to comfortable restrooms and rest areas. There are also wayside exhibits that explain historical perspectives and describe wildlife that may be seen along the way.

In 2001, the trail was named by USA Today one of the "10 great places to take a bike tour" in the world. The Pine Creek Gorge was also named a National Natural Landmark in 1968.

In 2015, the trail was named one of the ten best trails in Pennsylvania in a reader poll by the Rails-to-Trails Conservancy. The Pine Creek Rail-Trail was third only to the Great Allegheny Passage and the Allegheny River Trail.

Some people call this "an other world", one that occurs in a parallel universe. Twenty-first century luxuries co-exist alongside a rugged wilderness filled with wildlife and few modern interruptions. Areas of the rail-trail look virtually untouched from its early roots in the mid 1800's.

Spend a few hours here and it's easy to imagine the stories of bygone times. Come and join the ghosts of the past and me on a bike ride to remember.

PINE CREEK RAIL TRAIL ACCESS POINTS

ACCESS POINT	DISTANCE
Butler Road/Northern Terminus	0.0
Ansonia/Marsh Creek	7.3
Darling Run	8.7
Robert McCullough (Limited parking)	24.6
Rattlesnake Rock	26.4
Slate Run	35.2
Tomb Flats	36.2
Black Walnut Bottom	37.1
Clark Farm/Utceter Station	38.6
Ross Run	39.9
Waterville	50.1
Whitetail	59.1
Jersey Shore/Southern Terminus	62.0

See pages 185-200 for directions to the Trail Access Points.

STOKESDALE JUNCTION TO DARLING RUN

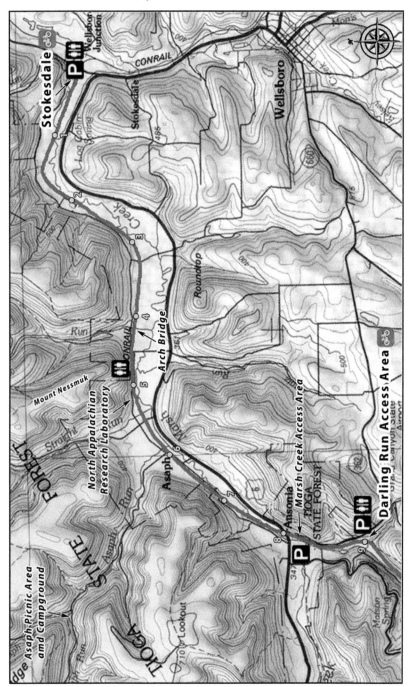

STOKESDALE JUNCTION TO DARLING RUN

1

This 8.7-mile section of the Pine Creek Rail-Trail starts at Stokesdale Junction, a hub for local railroads in the late 1800's. It follows the original rail bed along the Jersey Shore, Pine Creek, and Buffalo Railway, which traveled from Lyons, NY above Geneva, NY to Jersey Shore, PA (168.55 miles).

The ownership of this branch of the railroad changed hands several times over the next decades and eventually merged with the New York Central line in 1914, where it remained until Conrail took over in 1976. The last train ran this line on October 7, 1988.

Wellsboro Junction, also known as Stokesdale Junction was a busy area for just over a century. Now it is the terminal for the Wellsboro and Corning Railroad, a local freight system, as well as the Tioga Central Railroad, a local tourist train that runs between here and Tioga, PA. or Corning, NY.

Fog often lies in the marshes in the early morning on this section of the trail.

Starting at Stokesdale Junction, and along the length of the trail, we will find old railroad stone posts which mark the mileage from the original Lyons, NY headquarters. These are but one of the many remnants seen of the old rail system on the Rail-Trail. The stone posts have an "L" etched on them along with a mileage number. The first easily seen stone post is at Mile 6.5.

SEGMENT SUMMARY: This 8.7-mile section of the trail travels through a wide valley and wetland, past occasionally fog laden marshes and tiny towns.

A federal fish research laboratory is just off the trail and offers self-guided tours. There is an architecturally striking modern arched bridge along our way. The rail-trail passes the Marsh Creek access area where the horse and wagon tours join us on occasion. After pedaling under the highway bridge, we arrive at the confluence of Marsh Creek and Pine Creek. A short ways south is the Darling Run train station and access area.

The mileages in this book are shown in two ways. The first mileage is always the segment mileage; the overall mileage from the Northern Terminus is the second mileage listed.

Mile 0.0 Northern Terminus. Elevation 1175. The northern end of the Rail-Trail was added in 2007. This section of the trail follows a wide valley through farm lands and marshes. There is a temporary toilet "porta-john" at the parking lot.

Etiquette Rules are posted along the trail.

Often, there are maps of the Rail-Trail on the Information Board near the entrance to the Trail. Be sure to pick one up if some are there, as the maps are very helpful.

As you start to ride, please note the Bicycle Etiquette rules that are posted:

- Ride at a safe speed.
- Ride single file.
- Stay to the right.
- Alert others to your approach. (Saying "Coming up on your left" or something similar…is really helpful.)

This is a pack-it-in, carry-it-out trail. There are no garbage receptacles along the pathway.

A note of caution before you start to ride. There are no food or reliable water sources for the next 25 miles. The nearest store is in Blackwell, PA. Luckily, Pag-Omar Farms is near the entrance to the trail here. You may want to check it out for last minute nourishment.

We passed Pag-Omars on our way to the parking lot. They make excellent sandwiches and their ice cream is wonderful. They often have fresh grown vegetables and other local produce, including their own fresh grown corn in the summer. Their corn is some of the best around. Consider taking some home with you.

For those of you who geocache, there is one at Pag-Omars.. (Trail Treats, GC485PA)

At the entrance to the Trail, notice the bright yellow locked gate, which is meant to keep motorized traffic off the Rail-Trail.

Bicyclists may zip around the gate easily with a little balancing practice. The trail will have these gates at every intersection.

Summer colors and split rail fences on the trail.

At roadway intersections, DCNR rules state that bicyclists must stop at the gate before crossing the highway.

Be sure to notice the brown wooden mile markers that mark every mile along the trail. These markers track the mileage from here to the Southern Terminus. Be warned though that they are not totally accurate. At points they are almost .4 mile off.

Mile 0.9 (Mile 0.9) We see that Marsh Creek ambles alongside the trail through this section. It is a slow-flowing creek that has

Runners use the trail as much as bikers.
Dogs are often seen on the trail and must be leashed.

many curves and meanders. At times it will be relatively close to
the trail.

Other times, it may be up to 1/2 mile away. This section of the
trail follows a general southwest direction and parallels the RT.
6 highway to its south. You may hear the traffic far to our left.

We are traveling through a designated wetland area now.

Wetlands are defined as transitional areas between watered areas and land. The water table often lies at or close to the surface
here. Wetlands are known to benefit the waters of the area and
perform important cleansing functions. They also hold a diverse
wildlife population specific to marshlands.

This area of "The Muck" near the northern terminus of the trail
has been cited by Audubon PA as an "Important Birding Area".
There have been sightings of over 150 bird species in these wetlands.

The soils of the marshlands here are rich and wet. They were
once considered ideal for celery growing, but farming here de-
pended on the creation and maintenance of a fairly intensive
maze of drainage ditches. Not only did these economically un-

dermine the business, but they also changed the dynamics of the true marshland. Now there are restrictions on any altering of the structure of the wetlands.

Celery was a main-stay crop near this section of the trail.

Cultivating Celery at Wellsboro Junction, near Wellsboro. Pa.

This Postcard of celery growing at "The Muck" is courtesy of the Arlene Stager family.

Mile 3.0 (Mile 3.0) This spot is a perfect place to stop and watch for waterfowl. Sit on the bench and look for geese, ducks, herons, snapping turtles, and other wildlife.

Through the early summer months, you may even be able to see turtles laying eggs in nests along the trail. Just a reminder: Never approach wildlife or disturb their habitat. Be especially careful of snapping turtles, for although they are slow, their jaws are extremely dangerous.

A heron in the marshes near Mile 3.

A snapping turtle lays eggs right on the trail.

Mile 3.2 (Mile 3.2) Traveling south, watch for several road crossings in this section of the trail. All crossings are at grade, so be careful at each intersection as you go around the yellow gate and across the roadway. DCNR rules say that we are to stop first before riding across the road.

Mile 4.0 (Mile 4.0) Canada Run flows into Marsh Creek and this is the first of many short rail bridges along the trail. Most of the time there is barely any water in this small creek. But it is a good place to look for small, round, water-worn pebbles in the creek bed.

Red bee balm is a staple along streams during the summer months.

North of the trail, on our right, look to the largest mountain, Mt. Nessmuk, elevation, 2205.

WOODCRAFT
by
"Nessmuk"

Mt. Nessmuk is named for the 19th century outdoorsman, author, and conservationist George Washington Sears. (1821-1890). Sears gained fame writing for "Forest and Stream" magazine (later Field and Stream) He was only 5'3" and weighed 103 pounds.

He was an ultra-light camper and back-packer before his time. His solo canoe adventures included many self-guided trips, narrated through a series of letters titled "Rough Notes from the Woods."

At age 62 and in frail health at the time, Sears and his lightweight canoe, which he named the "Sary Gamp" (named after a Dickins character) finished a 266-mile journey through the central Adirondacks in New York state. The Sary Gamp is now owned by the Smithsonian Museum.

Sears used the pen name Nessmuk. His most famous book titled "Woodcraft and Camping" provided readers with instructions for outdoor skills.

His "Forest Runes" book of poems is equally excellent. Both books are now in the public domain and can still be downloaded online.

Nessmuk lived in Wellsboro and is buried in the cemetery there.

Nessmuk decried the destruction of the forests by the industrialization movement at the time, but never saw change prior to his death. He had great hope for us and this area though, as he wrote,

"But I think the next generation will see the better for it. The floods of a single season will sweep the streams clear of spent tan bark and poisonous chemicals. The denuded forests will be replaced. The dried up streams will be restocked and the wiser generation will conserve the game and fish instead of destroying them. Men will have learned something by that time…"

Historical marker on the "Green" in Wellsboro

As we pedal along, consider Nessmuk's wisdom about "Smoothing It", as opposed to "Roughing it."

"With a large majority of prospective tourists and outers, 'camping out' is a leading factor in the summer vacation. And during the long winter months they are prone to collect in little knots and talk much of camps, fishing, hunting, and 'roughing it.' The last phrase is very popular and always cropping up in the talks on matters pertaining to a vacation in the woods. I dislike the phrase. We do not go to the green woods and crystal waters to rough it, we go to smooth it. We get it rough enough at home; in towns and cities; in shops, offices, stores, banks and anywhere we may be placed - with the necessity always present on being on time and up to our work; of providing for the dependent ones; of keeping up, catching up, or getting left. Alas for the life-long battle, whose bravest slogan is bread."

- *George Washington Sears (Nessmuk): Woodcraft and Camping*

Mile 4.3 (Mile 4.3) We have arrived at the only arched bridge on the Rail-Trail. It spans the roadway below it. Its wooden planks are actually quieter than the sound of our tires riding over the gravel path. Up and over.

This is surprisingly, one of the steepest grades on the Rail-Trail. And it is jokingly referred to as one of the only hills on the trail.

The lower Marsh Creek arch bridge is a highlight of this section of the trail.

The arch bridge is not original to the rail bed.

The beauty of the bridge is not easily seen when you are on the trail itself. Consider taking a little path on the right to the roadway just before the bridge and riding the road to the bridge. You can easily backtrack to the path and continue on your way.

Mile 4.8.(Mile 4.8) Southwest of the bridge is a set of modern, stone-faced bathrooms, constructed by DCNR.

They smell better than most. This comfort station is equipped with skylights, a baby changing table, and a hand sanitizer dispenser.

The research laboratory is seen from the roadway just off the trail.

Mile 5.1 (Mile 5.1) At the intersection of the Strait Run Road sits the Northern Appalachian Research Laboratory, owned and run by the United States Geological Survey.

This branch houses a research facility to study aquatic biology. Some past studies have included genetic variations of salmon, the impact of freshwater mussels on water quality, and the impact of the return of eels to their native habitat. The property has an outdoor raceway system, wet and dry labs, library, and a conference center.

The research laboratory is not visible from the rail-trail, but a quick right turn at the roadway crossing brings us to the lab. Self-tours are available.

Annually, in mid-September the parking lots at the Laboratory become a hub of activity. A mountain bike race is held in the

Dame's Rockets are the purple flowers seen in June all along the trail.

mountains behind here in early September. And around the same time, an ultra-marathon is held on the rail-trail over a weekend. The start-finish lines are here at the Laboratory.

Mile 5.7 (Mile 5.7) After crossing the road, the trail skirts a small village at the base of the mountains. This is the tiny town of Asaph, PA.

The village of Asaph glows in the early morning sunlight as fog hangs above. We look north, back the way we came, in this photo.

By car, folks can follow the road from Asaph towards Asaph Picnic area and Campground, a very rustic and isolated small landing in the mountains. This is the site of one of the spectator areas for the Susquehannock Trail Performance Rally, held annually. Race cars drive race speeds on forestry roads throughout the region. The Asaph site is always one for sliding turns and sometimes off-road travel.

The Asaph Wild Area is north of the town. No improvements are allowed in Wild Areas to protect their undeveloped setting.

Mile 6.5 (Mile 6.5) This is the first of many stone mileage markers we will see on the Trail. This one signifies that we are 113 miles from Lyons, NY, headquarters of the old New York Central Railroad. The railroad in the late 1800's installed stone markers along the entire mileage of the trail. Sadly, many are now missing, especially on the northern sec-

One of the original mileage markers to our right as we ride south, just off the trail path.

tions of the trail. These old markers are actually more accurate than the wooden modern mileage markers we see.

Mile 7.3 (Mile 7.3) We have arrived at the **Marsh Creek access area.**

Ansonia has a storied railroad past. It was a connecting point for the railways that traveled east and west as well as for the railroad that traveled through the Pine Creek Gorge.

There is parking access to the trail here as well as easy access

A horse drawn wagon pulls into the tour driveway as I ride by one day.

to a wagon ride that travels the rail bed part way through the canyon. Be careful here and watch for large wagons pulled by draft horses.

From this point south, the trail splits into two tracks, with the right-hand track heading south reserved for horse traffic. There will be plenty of horse manure here to negotiate as well as elevation changes between the two tracks.

The original railroad yards where multiple track sidings lay in the late 1800's and early 1900's were north of the double bridge, at the current parking area.

Compare these pictures with what we can see now and pause a moment to listen for "ghostly whispers".

These old postcards were photographed by Nelson A. Caulkins. Caulkins documented many scenes of the entire rail-trail area in the early 1900's. They are courtesy of Joyce Tice and the History Center on Main Street, Mansfield, PA.

One hundred and thirty years ago, train whistles blew, steam engines chugged, and people bustled as a part of life in Ansonia on this very spot.

From the bridge, looking south, the old church in the postcard is still visible.

The rail bridges in the old photo are still here. The bridge picture looks north and east, back towards Asaph. The depot in the background sat aside the current parking area and former track sidings.

Settlers originally called this little town "Manchester Farms". But af-

A logger's shack at Pine Woods, near Ansonia.

27

ter most of the lands were purchased by Anson Phelps for his sawmills, it was renamed Ansonia. The year after the railroad finished, the old hotel was erected and the town saw more activity.

Historically, Ansonia pre-dates the coming of the railroads by thousands of years, as the large flat lands in this area were originally named "Big Meadows" by the "Kanonsionni", the name the peoples of the Iroquois Nation used for themselves. It reportedly meant "People of the Longhouse". They had a village here.

Philip Tome, son of an early settler of the Pine Creek area of Lycoming County was a hunter and outdoorsman who wrote a book in 1854 titled, "Pioneer Life or Thirty Years a Hunter".

In the book he documents,

> *"...In 1794 James King and a Mr. Manning went on an exploring expedition up Pine Creek, to ascertain if any elk were to be found, and also if any Indians were in the neighborhood.*
>
> *They ascended that stream in a canoe and about the seventh or eighth day after starting arrived at the third fork of Pine Creek.*
>
> *On the west side, opposite the fork, they discovered a large tract of cleared land, consisting of as many as a hundred and sixty acres, to which they gave the name of Big Meadows.*
>
> *They were the first white men there. It had been cleared by the Six Nations. On the opposite side of the creek, near the fork, they found a plain orchard of twenty acres, abounding with fruit. Between the plum orchard and the creek was a tract of cleared land of about thirty acres, which appeared to have once been a cornfield. In this vicinity, they "found a great many elk and bears..."*

The large fields of Big Meadows, the area along RT. 6 at Ansonia, are still a hotbed for Indian artifacts. After spring rains, especially, you may see local arrowhead hunters frequenting the plowed fields in search of artifacts.

The Pine Creek Gorge became an early path for members of these First American tribes. Some scholars believe the Path followed the exact track bed we are following through the gorge area. Others believe that the upper gorge, because of its steep mountain sides, deep forests, and fast running waters was considered taboo by these early tribes who considered it a resting place for spirits.

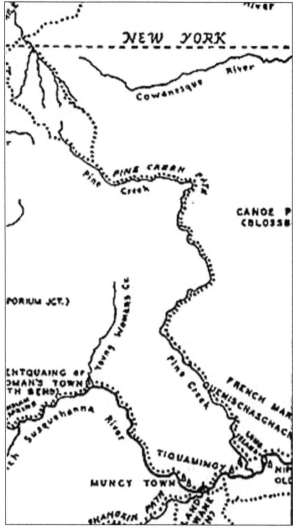

A portion of an old map from the Internet showing the Pine Creek Path.

At any rate, it is not contested that parts of this trail are in fact a pre-railroad means of transportation for tribal people as well as early settlers.

The path was used by the Seneca and later by Iroquois warriors who traveled to points south and to the Great Shamokin Path, the major east-west route in central Pennsylvania. At times, it was a means to accomplish war raids. One of the earliest accounts of

29

This historical marker sits at the intersection of RT. 6 and RT. 362, near the Ansonia bridge.

the path is by Moses Van Campen, who was captured in 1782 and taken north along the path as a prisoner.

Even until the War of 1812, there were bands of warriors who lived in the Gorge along the path.

The Iroquois called the Ansonia - Big Meadows area the Third Fork of the Path.

It's time for a short geology lesson here. This is the spot that Marsh Creek and Pine Creek merge and start a southern flow through what is known as Pennsylvania's Grand Canyon, an area with mountain walls as high as 1000 feet above the path and creek.

Many rocks found near the bottom of the Pine Creek Gorge contain fossils of ancient brachiopods. Some of these fossils point to this whole area being submerged beneath deep waters. Some of the rock outcrops at the top of the Gorge date back at least 300 million years, although the Gorge itself is about 20,000 years old.

Pine Creek had flowed northeasterly originally, but had been dammed by soil, ice, rocks, and debris deposited there by the receding Laurentide Continental Glacier. The dammed creek formed a lake at Ansonia-Big Meadows. This lake sat in an east - west direction with no outlet through the Gorge. During the movement of the glaciers, the advancing ice spilled over in this area and started flooding the area to the south, along Pine Creek,

The highway bridge along RT. 6 is pretty in all seasons. We pass under it.

This wall of water eroded the deep channel we now see. This on-going action—glacial advances and retreats, eroded Pine Creek to the point that the southern flow became permanent.

Imagine that the highest outcrops at the top of the Gorge were once the coastline of the shallow sea that once covered most of

The "Blue Moon" at pre-dawn one morning at the confluence of Pine Creek and Marsh Creek.

31

North America. At Barbour Rocks, high on the rim of the gorge, there are huge rocks with fossilized ripple marks carved on them.

Fossils are especially noticeable near the Turkey Path, in Leonard Harrison State Park and in the creek itself.

Mile 8.0 (Mile 8.0) South of the highway bridge, wc get our first look at Pine Creek. Pine Creek and Marsh Creek merge and head south. This is a particularly tranquil section of the Pine Creek Trail.

An adult eagle at Darling Run.

Look for eagles in this area. The long row of pines on the other side of Pine Creek often hosts sitting eagles while they watch for fish in the creek.

There will often be Canada geese here, too.

On occasion, there will be fly fishermen in the creek. Pine Creek is well known for its water sports and is designated a "Water Trail". The Pennsylvania Fish and Game Commission manages this area and stocks trout along over 56 miles of the stream. According to PA Angler and Boater magazine, Pine Creek has more miles stocked with

Folks pointing at an eagle sitting in a tree just above them.

trout than any other stream in Pennsylvania. There are many native fishes in Pine Creek also, mostly brook and brown trout.

The upper areas of the Pine Creek Gorge provide excellent trout fishing. Along the lower sections of the Trail, warm water fish await, including small mouth bass, walleye, rock bass, as well as trout.

We should notice the water level in the creek, which varies depending on the time of the year. During the spring months, the water flow is brisk. We may see canoeists, rafters and kayakers in the creek moving along at a quick pace. By June, the water levels begin to drop and the pace is much more leisurely. Inner tubes are the preferred watercraft during the summer months.

However, in the spring especially, there are a few sections of the Gorge that have Class II and III rapids. Boaters are always advised to assess the situation and should portage around the rapids, if necessary.

By August, paddling is, for all intents and purposes, done. Fish are lingering only in deep holes in the stream, now.

One day when I was biking in this area, two women were taking pictures of something in the creek. When I asked them, they

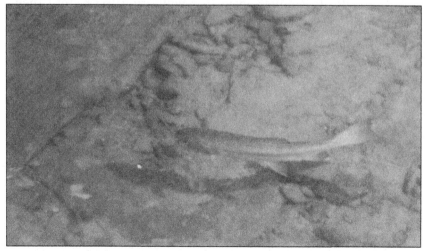

This is a large rainbow trout in the bottom of a creek bed. They have a red stripe.

pointed out a large brown trout taking flies off the surface of the stream. There would be a huge splash as the fish came mostly up out of the water to eat the nymph fly.

Mile 8.5 (Mile 8.5) We are approaching the **Darling Run access area** now. The little train station building houses a small museum of items, but is often closed. On weekends, we may be lucky to see volunteers who are in the area and available to answer questions and perhaps even point out an eagle. The station is open when they are here.

There is an active eagle nest in the area, so you may see the resident eagles anywhere here. There are adults with the traditional white head and tail as well as brown and mottled brown juveniles here and in the Pine Creek Gorge.

A word of caution: Please do not disturb the eagles, especially during nesting season in the spring and early summer.

This is an especially fragile time in the eagles' lifespans. Once the eggs hatch in April, the eaglets will be regularly fed by both parents until they fledge at 12 weeks of age, usually in mid-June.

Any disturbance in the area could result in danger for or even abandonment of the eaglets. Parents will continue to bring food to the fledged juveniles, even in neighboring trees, until they learn to hunt on their own. Eaglets   learn to hunt quickly so activity around the nest dies down drastically by mid-August.

Eagles regularly fly up and down the creek, hunting. Listen carefully, because eagles call to one another and it's usually a good way to locate one. Their call has been described as a high-pitched gull-like cackle.

We may be able to catch sight of the nest here. Just north of the train station is a brown wooden marker identifying "Cole Furman Run." Stop just north of this marker in the first open area, where there are few trees between the trail and Pine Creek. The opposite shore should be clearly visible now.

An eaglet in the Darling Run eagle nest.

Across the creek, on the creek flat, is a large white pine tree mixed among other deciduous trees. It is quite a ways away. About two-thirds up the pine tree will be the large nest. The nest has been in this location for years. Each year the adult eagles add new materials to the nest in order to ready it for raising a new family. That's why the nest is so large.

Eels are another interesting resident of the Pine Creek Gorge. The American eel is a skinny, long, fish-like creature with a fused dorsal fin. Although they look snakelike, they are harmless. Eels used to migrate yearly from the Chesapeake Bay, but have been blocked by the large dams on the Susquehanna River. Young eels were captured below the dams and transported here to continue their lifespan in these home waters.

Eels are hosts for mussels which help purify the waters of Pine Creek. The story is detailed at the interpretive panel next to the old train station.

Mile 8.7 (Mile 8.7) Restrooms, also known as comfort stations, are available at the **Darling Run access area**. There is also ample parking. Although there is no cell phone service here, there is an outdoor telephone near the comfort station that can be used to make free local calls.

Look for maps of the entire Rail-Trail at the interpretive panel. They are very informative. And be sure to read the interesting information on the kiosk.

Now is a good time to talk about Pine Creek. We may think sometimes it looks very much like a river, but it's not. It's always Pine CREEK. And the locals often pronounce it Pine CRICK.

DARLING RUN TO TIADAGHTON

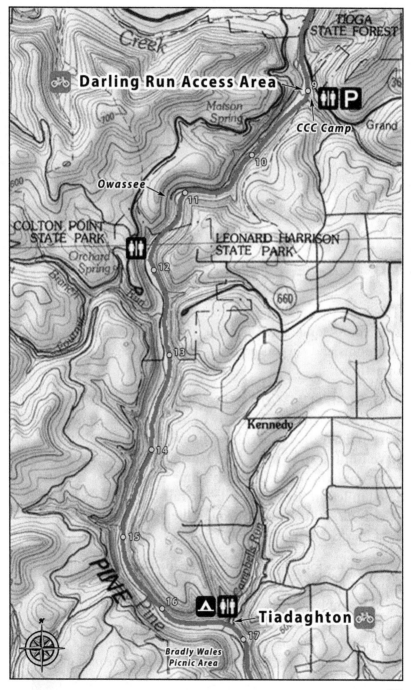

2

DARLING RUN TO TIADAGHTON

The Pine Creek Rail-Trail continues on at Darling Run, just south of Ansonia, PA. There is a large access area here, including restrooms and several parking areas. (See page 188 for driving directions)

SEGMENT SUMMARY: This 7.4-mile segment of the Pine Creek Rail-Trail is frequently described as the most beautiful part of the trail. Local riders often suggest this ride if you only have limited time for a trip. However, this segment isn't for everyone. These are arguably some of the most remote, isolated miles on the Rail-Trail. The rail-trail follows Pine Creek closely as it cuts its way through the bottom of an 800 to 1000 foot gorge.

There is no food or reliable water for the next 16 miles. This segment ends at a ghost town with limited modern driving access. It simply ends in the middle of nowhere. You must decide before leaving here if you will turn around in Tiadaghton and return to Darling Run or whether you will continue to ride to Blackwell, another 8.3 miles and equally desolate part of the trail.

There is no easy access to or exit from the trail for the next 16 miles of the Trail. (Until Blackwell.)

The mileages in this book are shown in two ways. The first mileage is always the segment mileage; the overall mileage from the Northern Terminus is the second mileage listed.

Mile 0.0 (Mile 8.7) From Darling Run to Tiadaghton, the trail moves into the Pine Creek Gorge, an isolated, beautifully wild area of the Rail-Trail that follows Pine Creek on its eastern shore.

The sides of the mountains encroach more closely as they also rise higher and higher through this section. At the State Parks, we will be 835 feet below the ledges that loom above us. Further south, near Waterville, the trail is 1450 feet below the rim of the Canyon.

The Darling Run train station is used as a little museum now. If it is open, be sure to go inside and look at some of the pictures there. There is also an interpretive panel, right on the trail, with interesting information about the history of this location.

When the railroad first opened, there were 32 railway stations along the 78-mile rail bed from Stokesdale to Williamsport. The July 12, 1883 Williamsport paper reported that the railroad had "an eye for high art" because its stations were built after the Swiss cottage style of architecture.

Take a look at the two trails, side by side, at Darling Run. The raised, stone trail is for bikers and hikers. The dirt pathway is for the horses that pull the wagon ride that takes tours partway into the Gorge. We may see one of the tour wagons as we pass through. If we don't see the horses in person, be sure to check out the size of their hooves as they leave prints in the dirt. Also, be careful because there is horse manure in abundance along the horse side of the trail. The horse trail runs from Ansonia to Tiadaghton.

Looking south at the Darling Run station, the interpretive panel and the trail.

A word of caution about the two side-by-side trail beds. Moving from one side to the other on a bike can be tricky because of loose gravel and the slight difference in elevation.

It's time to keep watch for wildlife. There is an eagle nest in the vicinity and often the Darling Run eagle pair can be spotted here. See pages 34-35 for nest location.

If we are here on Sunday, often the volunteer at the train station will have a telescope and can help point out any eagles perched in the trees.

One Sunday, we were visiting and the volunteer pointed out an eagle just off the trail. Often the only thing that catches your attention is a white point in the trees. Eagles very rarely perch close enough to see them well with the naked eye. And with their super eyesight, they will be in flight long before you can get close.

There have been many occasions I have seen an eagle take flight in front of me on the trail, long before I get there. They will often fly along the stream and into the trees on the opposite side of Pine Creek.

Mile 0.3 (Mile 9.0) This is the site of the Darling Run Civilian Conservation Corps (CCC) camp (Company 1354, S-155-

Recumbent trikes are often seen on the trail.

Asaph). The Civilian Conservation Corps was the brainchild of President Franklin D. Roosevelt and was an attempt to get people back to work after the Great Depression of the 1930's.

Forty-five days after Roosevelt took office the first enrollees were accepted into what became known as the CCC. Nationwide, the CCC was in existence from 1933 to 1942.

This is what the Leonard Harrison State Park website has to say about the CCC years:

Unmarried, unemployed men age 18-25 were the first enrollees. Later, the age limit changed to 17-23. World War I veterans also had separate camps. Enrollment was for six months and could be extended up to a total of two years.

Many young men came to the camps hungry and poorly clothed. They were issued uniforms and given three meals a day. Most young men gained about 40 pounds while in the CCC. The men earned $30 a month, most of which was sent home to their families.

Run by the U.S. Army, the regimented life of camp was new to most new enrollees. A typical day began at 6 A.M. with breakfast at 6:30 A.M. followed by sick call and policing of the camp. At

The sign on the trail at the CCC site. The camp was just south of the Darling Run stream, on the side of the creek.

7:15 A.M. trucks were loaded with tools and men for the day. "Local experienced men" usually served as foremen for the work. Lunch was usually half of an hour. At 4 P.M. the trucks headed back to camp for the flag lowering ceremony, inspection, and announcements.

After dinner, the men had free time until lights out at 10 P.M.

The U.S. Army ran the camps, but foresters, carpenters, and other people directed the work. The CCC fought forest fires, planted trees, built roads, buildings, picnic areas, swimming areas, campgrounds and created many state parks. When not working, the men socialized and had opportunities to learn crafts and skills.

Each camp had about 200 men, including an army officer and junior officer, camp doctor, educational advisor, and the project supervisor.

The average camp had about 24 buildings, including kitchen, mess hall, barracks and quarters for the officers. Many camps began as tent cities until the permanent camp could be built.

Pennsylvania had 151 CCC camps, the second largest in the nation.

The Darling Run CCC camp is credited with providing projects over 27,000 acres. Their projects consisted of road construction, game protection, blister rust control, and forest management in the area.

Colton Point and Leonard Harrison State Parks, the two parks on the upper ledges of both sides of the Pine Creek Gorge have several pavilions, buildings, and pathways that were built by this CCC camp. In 1988, the five pavilions at Colton Point State Park were added to the National Register of Historic Places.

At Leonard Harrison State Park, there is a bronze monument dedicated to CCC workers and the work they did in the area.

The statue at Leonard Harrison State Park.

Once a year, the State Park hosts a CCC veterans' reunion for those who were stationed at the CCC camps in the state. Many of the veterans are now in their nineties.

This old photo can be seen inside the Darling Run train station. It is used here courtesy of Mike Cooney and Ann Benjamin, "Wellsboro", Arcadia Publishing.

This is a rare picture of the actual Darling Run CCC.

Off the trail at Darling Run is an old dynamite shack in the woods.

There is some disagreement about whether it was the storage shack for the TNT for the CCC camp or for the railroad. TNT was always stored far in the woods, so that if it blew up, nothing was damaged.

The old TNT shack on Darling Run.

Mile 0.8 (Mile 9.5)
As we relax on the

smooth, level path, it might be interesting to look at the people who frequent the Rail-Trail. Many bicycles can be seen here. Most are hybrid types of bicycles, with a mix of mountain bike and road bike features. Some are recumbent bikes and trikes.

There are plenty of bicycle trailers and many families with children who ride a variety of bikes.

Mile 1.2 (Mile 9.9) Owassee Slide Run also known as Chimney Hollow flows to Pine Creek across the stream from the

This is a little one whose mom let me take her picture one day.

Trail. According to Chuck Dillon, local historian and author, it got its name because there was an early settlement high on the mountain. The town couldn't be seen from the railroad bed, but smoke coming from the houses' chimneys could be seen. The area became "Chimney Hollow".

This area is covered with an understory of ferns, mountain laurel, and striped maple, also known as Moosewood. Ferns grow quickly and rob the ground underneath of sunlight, water, and minerals. They also secrete chemicals that prevent hardwood seedlings from growing.

The West Rim Trail high on the canyon rim crosses Owassee Slide Run on a wooden footbridge. (Description courtesy of Chuck Dillon, "Explore Pa's Grand Canyon: Short Hikes in the Tioga State Forest)

Owassee Slide Run is the site of one of the Gorge's log slides, during the lumber era. The log slide was used on a year-round basis: during the winter the logs slid down on ice; following the snowmelt the slide was greased to ease the descent of the logs.

The logs were then loaded onto rafts and arks and floated downstream.

Keep looking for wildlife here. This is pristine territory and there is little human access to the Gorge from this point on, except via the creek and the rail-trail. The road across from us is a dead end that goes to some private cabins along the stream.

A photo I took of an osprey eating a fish.

We may see ospreys. Ospreys had been endangered in Pennsylvania because of the effects of DDT poisoning. In 1986, the first reintroduced ospreys successfully nested in the county. Since then, there are several nests along local waterways.

One day, I was across the stream from here and an osprey carrying a large fish in his talons flew over me and north towards Darling Run!

Headed south, Pinafore Run is on the left, Muskrat Eddy is on our right, and Snyder Point/Kennedy Point is ahead of us.

SUNRISE IN THE
FOREST

*The zephyrs of
morning are
stirring the
larches,
And, lazily
lifting, the mist
rolls away.
A paean of
praise thro' the
dim forest
arches.
Is ringing, to
welcome the
advent of day.
Is loftily
ringing,
Exultingly
ringing,
From the height
where a little
brown songster
is clinging
To the
top of a
hemlock, the
uttermost spray.*

Mile 1.5 (Mile 10.2) We will pass one of the few camps in the Canyon. Look now, on our side of the Canyon, near the Pinafore Run sign, for the hill known as Snyder Point. For a long time, this was the furthest south in the canyon anyone lived. The Alexander Kennedy family had a home high on the mountain for many years. In truth, the point should be called Kennedy Point, because the Kennedy family lived here long before the Snyders.

In the early years of the marketing of the "Grand Canyon of Pennsylvania", Larry Woodin, a Wellsboro businessman, organized tourism photographs to be taken from this mountain. According to Scott Gitchell, a relative of the Kennedys, opening scene backdrops for the 1940's movie, "Unconquered" starring Gary Cooper were shot here.

The Civilian Conservation Corps planted large red pine plantations high on this mountain.

Pinafore Run, where it exits here under the rail-trail is also known as "Muskrat Eddy", one of Nessmuk's favorite camping spots.

Nessmuk reportedly wrote some of his Forest Runes poetry while camping here.

I often think of Nessmuk's poem titled "Sunrise in the Forest" when I ride through here early in the morning.

To read about Nessmuk, check out Section 1 of this book.

Looking to our right, the rock ledge is Barbour Rocks. With binoculars, we can see the overlooks of the Barbour Rock trail, right on the cliff's edge.

Mile 1.8 (Mile 10.5) Barbour Rock, elevation 1962, is a rampart of red sandstone cliffs. It stands high above us on the west side (on the right, headed south) of the creek. This red ledge is said to be a part of the Catskill Formation of the Upper Devonian Age.

These sedimentary rocks are about 350 million years old. (Dillon) The red color is caused by the presence of oxidized iron, caused when the rocks met the waters of the original sea here.

Near Railroad Mile marker L-117 on the left, is one of the few places on the rail-trail where there is a cell phone signal. It is fleeting, but good enough for texts.

Stone markers like this one were installed at each mile of the old railroad. This one signifies that we are 117 miles from Lyons, NY, headquarters of the Old New York Central Railroad.

The Barbour Rock Trail, off the Colton Point Road is a beautiful mile-long handicap accessible trail that brings hikers to the Canyon edge. There are few barriers at the end of the trail which ends at cliff's edge. Hikers are cautioned here because non-handicapped parts of the trail are narrow, full of tree roots, and very close to the canyon's edge. This is one of the most unobstructed,

High above us, the sign for the Barbour Rocks Trail sits on the Colton Road.

unspoiled, unimproved views anywhere in the Gorge.

On the Rail-Trail below, something to be aware of is that people will be watching us from above through this entire section from here to south of the Turkey Path.

Barbour Rock is named for Samuel Barbour, who was killed in a log jam just below this point.

Pine Creek has a storied history with the logging business before and during the time of the railroads. Shipbuilders believed that the white pine trees of the Pine Creek Gorge afforded the very best lumber available for making ship's masts. Three white pine spars, each 90 feet long were fastened end to end to make a single clipper ship mast. Each spar must be straight and strong.

Pine Creek provided exactly what the ship-builders wanted and so trees were felled up

A typical log raft

49

and down the gorge. Each tree would be cut to fall as gingerly as possible and then was lashed to other trees to form a log raft that was then floated in the spring down Pine Creek to the Susquehanna River and subsequently to the Chesapeake Bay.

Navigating the heavy rafts in the swift flowing stream required agility and a good deal of bravery on the loggers' parts.

By 1840, it is said that almost 500 rafts, containing millions of board feet of lumber, floated down the Pine Creek Gorge.

However, by 1879, the log rafting business ceased and instead, clear cutting the forest became vogue.

Now individual logs were dammed behind artificial dams and then released en masse towards their southern destinations. It was hard dangerous work for loggers on Pine Creek.

An area splash dam. There were many of these along Pine Creek.

Samuel Barbour was just one of many who lost their lives here as part of the lumber industry. The death of Barbour is chronicled in a delightful book, titled, "Flatlanders and Ridgerunners: Folktales from the Mountains" by James Glimm. Glimm retells many of the old folklore stories of the region in this book.

By the late 1880's, many businesses came to believe that it was more economical to bring logs to sawmill via the railroad rather than river floating.

A gear-driven Shay locomotive on the Leetonia narrow gauge railway.(Photo courtesy of Lori-jo Stoner)

The main rail bed existed here where we are riding, but there also were numerous small-scale, narrow gauge railroads built along the upper ledges of the Gorge. Some of the railroads connected with the trains at the bottom of the Gorge via high trestles and switch-backed rail beds down the side of the mountains, but others used log slides in this area to transport the logs to the base of the Gorge.

This old Victorian postcard was probably taken from Barbour Rocks. Note the railroad bed next to Pine Creek, just as it is now.

One of the lumbermen who owned much of the land on the east side of the Gorge, (our left, heading south) was Leonard Harrison, who donated many of his lands to the state in 1922 for what

A Shay locomotive at Colton Point. Notice the almost clear-cut mountainside.

is now Leonard Harrison State Park, just a little further to our south.

Likewise, the lands around Colton Point Lookout on the other side of the canyon were heavily logged by the William Wilkins Company, Silas Billings, and later Henry Colton. Colton's land was later deeded to the State in the early 1900's and became Colton Point State Park.

If you are interested in learning more about the logging industry in this area, the Pennsylvania Lumberman's Museum, west of the village of Galeton on RT. 6 has thousands of relics and tells the story of the lumberman's life. A CCC cabin is reconstructed on site. There is also a full-size Shay locomotive, similar to those used in the Gorge, on display there.

Some of the original narrow gauge logging railroad beds were later converted by the CCC in the 1930's into forestry roads and hiking trails after the railroads were abandoned.

Mile 2.1 (Mile 10.8) Just south of Barbour Rock is Barbour Bend, also known as Owassee. Owassee is the Iroquois name for rapids.

The rapids cannot be seen from the Rail-Trail. As you approach an island, the stream splits. The far side of the island is the main stream bed. There is a short stretch of rapids here. We may hear the noise as we approach, especially in the spring.

(Photos courtesy of Jon Dillon, Pine Creek Outfitters)

At times, these rapids approach Class III in strength. Class III rapids are defined as being difficult, with waves, rocks, and rapids. Advanced maneuvering skills are recommended.

Through the years, there have been deaths of rafters, kayakers, or canoeists in this section of the Gorge. Proper equipment and a good guide are imperative.

Mile 2.3 (Mile 11.0) The suspension bridge and camp here signify the end of the stretch of rapids just to the north. Many folks beach their watercraft here, drain out the water, change into dry clothes, and re-tell the harrowing account of the brief, but unremitting gantlet of the rapids.

Near the suspension bridge, look back to the north. The rapids are more than likely just a placid part of the stream right now. Look for the large rock on the other side of the far fork in the stream. It's the same rock as shown in the picture of the rafters.

We may see activity at the camp. It's an enviable place to visit.

The camp is on one of two small parcels of private land within the parks. Please be considerate of private boundaries.

Mile 2.6 (Mile 11.3) In this vicinity is Split Rock Ledge. Pine Creek narrows in this part of the canyon, which causes faster water to flow along the trail here. The bedrock ledge in the stream is called Split Rock. When standing in the creek, folks may see splotches of paint covering many of the larger rocks, where canoes, especially, have scraped when the water is low. At high water times, the ledge is covered and the water runs quickly, pushing boaters up against the high walls above. But during low water, the rock ledge is exposed and creates a small mini falls in the creek. A quick hike to the creek, off a path near the bench and then downstream through the creek will bring us there. It is tricky footing and a treacherous walk through the creek.

Colton Point Lookout can be seen from the rail-trail.

Looking up to the west, high on the mountain, across the creek, we may glimpse Colton Point Lookout. Look carefully because it is partially hidden, tucked into the upper part of the tree-sided mountain.

Colton Point Lookout

We may glimpse the glint of the metal viewers and railing at the lookout. Watch for the bench by the trail on our right. The lookout is directly overhead now. We will get a better glimpse of it down the trail a bit, near the restroom.

Leonard Harrison Lookout

A careful search in front of us, to our left, may also give a view of the Leonard Harrison Outlook to the south.

55

Mile 2.8 (Mile 11.5) This is the northern boundary of Leonard Harrison and Colton Point State Parks. On the accompanying map we can see that we are now at the "Grand Canyon of Pennsylvania".

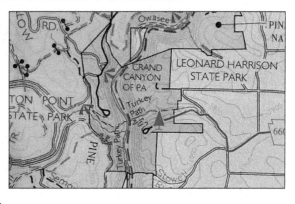

The Pine Creek Gorge National Natural Landmark includes Colton Point and Leonard Harrison State Parks and parts of the Tioga State Forest along 12 miles of Pine Creek between Ansonia and Blackwell. The Gorge is also protected by the state of Pennsylvania as the 12,163 acre Pine Creek Gorge Natural Area, which is the second largest State Natural Area in Pennsylvania. Both Parks are designated a State Park Natural Area.

These overlooks offer easily accessed modern viewing platforms for the Pine Creek Gorge below them. Leonard Harrison State Park is more developed than Colton Point, but both offer spectacular views of the Canyon. Leonard Harrison Park has a concession stand and small visitors center that are open for limited hours.

Both State Parks have camping sites available. More amenities are found at Leonard Harrison Park.

Mile 3.1 (Mile 11.8) We have arrived at another set of DCNR installed modern, stone-faced comfort stations, also known as pit toilets.

To see Colton Point Lookout from here, stand next to the restroom, turn around and face north. Look for the small rock outcrop high on the mountain. We may see the glint of the viewers there.

Mile 3.5 (Mile 12.2) The double bridges at the Turkey Paths signify the endpoints of two hiking paths that travel up each side

of the Gorge here. The DCNR mile marker at the bridge says Mile 12.

On the west side of the Gorge, the Colton Point Turkey Path follows a moderate to steep slope for 1.25 miles over 570 feet elevation. This trail is accessed by fording the stream. It lacks the stairs and boardwalks of the Leonard Harrison Turkey Path.

The Leonard Harrison Turkey Path descends right to the Rail-Trail. This footpath follows Little Fourmile Run for a mile in length over 830 feet in ascent. The Turkey Path was built upon the remains of a path used during the logging era.

Park your bike at the bike rack and hike at least a little ways up the trail to sense the wooden walkways and stairs built in 1978 and 1985 by the Pennsylvania Youth Conservation Corps.

At the base of the trail is a waterfall. There are several waterfalls before the Leonard Harrison Turkey Path bears to the right and ascends to the lookout at the top of the Gorge. We can also see the forest change from a mixed oak to northern hardwoods on the trail.

At the waterfalls and near Pine Creek notice some of the rocks that contain ripple marks of waves from over 250 million years ago when this area was a large continental sea. A sharp look may show fossilized sea creatures, rushes, and ferns.

A fossil rock at the base of the Turkey Path.

It is illegal to remove fossils, so please don't.

Many times there is only a little water at the waterfalls, depending on the water level overall in the Canyon.

A word of caution: Stay on the marked trails when hiking in the Canyon. These are steep climbs and the trail can be quite slippery when wet. Shortcuts also hasten erosion, so please do not cross any switchbacks on the trails.

At the base of the Turkey Path, there is a bike rack and bench.

This is a perfect place to explore for a while. A quick hike up the Turkey Path trail is a fun diversion. A hike down the tiny path to Pine Creek gives folks a chance to easily wade in the stream in

The two camps on either side of Fourmile Run. (Photo courtesy of Ruhrfisch, Wiki Commons)

times of low water. (The stream bed is slippery, so falls are likely. The best way to hike across is to bring a pair of old sneakers and wear them in the water.)

A gentle reminder about safety: People have been hurt and there have even been drownings in this area. Emergency help is not easily available. There is no cell service here. The only way to get help is to climb the Leonard Harrison Turkey Path and seek out someone to assist. Emergency personnel must access this area from Tiadaghton, four miles to the south or Darling Run, almost four miles to our north. Emergency response times, by the nature of the isolation here are extended.

On one weekend in August 2015, there were two evacuations from this area. On Saturday, a visitor had an ankle injury near the base of the Turkey Path. The next day a woman went into premature labor a little higher on the Turkey Path, after having come to the rail-trail here. In both cases, emergency personnel were called and evacuations were made. The process took hours.

Visitors sometimes build rock art in the creek, marking this serene and isolated place. There is also a trail marker cairn in the water between the two Turkey Paths. The cairns clearly mark this area when looking from above.

Across Pine Creek is another section of private land. Please be considerate of private boundaries.

Mile 3.6 (Mile 12.3) There are two camps on either side of Four-mile Run, across the creek from the Rail-Trail. The camp that is north of Fourmile Run is one of two that were built in the heart of the Pine Creek Gorge in the 1900's by Leonard Harrison. He named his original camps "Wetumka" and "Osocosy".

The other camp here, to the south of Fourmile Run, was built sometime after 1903 by Pennsylvania Governor William Stone, a Wellsboro native. He named it "Heart's Ease". Governor Stone frequently visited his cabin, arriving by train at a railroad stop near the foot of the Turkey Path. President Theodore (Teddy) Roosevelt is said to have stayed here and fished Fourmile Run behind the camp, one of his favorite places to fish.

Some of Roosevelt's trips here may have helped formulate his vision for a national park system in the U.S. After he became President in 1901, Roosevelt used his authority to protect wildlife and public lands by creating the U.S. Forest Service and establishing 51 Federal Bird Reservations, four National Game Preserves, 150 National Forests, five National Parks and enabling the 1906 American Antiquities Act which he used to proclaim 19 National Monuments. During his presidency, Theodore Roosevelt protected approximately 230,000 acres of public land.

Although Fourmile Run will probably have little water in it if we visit between June and September, it is a superb stream for native trout fishing. There is a rugged trail that follows the stream bed to the Painter–Leetonia Road, above, that entails scrambling past several waterfalls. Many pools of water have fish in them.

A reminder: A fishing license is required to fish in any stream or waterway in Pennsylvania. Limits and regulations are specified.

According to Chuck Dillon's description of Fourmile Run,

> *"Just about any pool will contain native trout, but they disappear quickly when they see you or sense your footsteps. If you*

are fishing, use a red worm, walk softly, and remain hidden as you let the worm bounce down the stream into a pool or past an eddy. If you catch one, wet your hands before removing the hook so that you do not remove the fish's protective mucous coating when you release it."

Fourmile Run is designated a Wild Stream under the Pennsylvania Wild and Scenic Rivers System. As Dillon reminds us, "Its fragile ecology and continued health of the stream depends upon your proper behavior—keep sticks, trash, and excess debris from entering and muddying the water."

Mile 3.7 (Mile 12.4) Above us, the Overlook Trail footpath works its way to Otter View, 2/3 of a mile south high above us at Leonard Harrison State Park.

The view at Otter View Vista.

A careful search of the mountain behind us, to our north, may point out the barricade at Otter View Vista. It has a white fence.

Mile 3.9 (Mile 12.6) Railroad marker L-119 is here. This one signifies that we are 119 miles from Lyons, NY, headquarters of the old New York Central Railroad. These old stone markers are accurate. There are fewer on the upper end of the trail than on the southern end. They should be found on every mile of the railbed.

Looking up at Otter View Vista.

In this area of the Gorge, river otters were released in the early 1980's, as part of a project to reintroduce these native mammals into their original habitat. River otters once flourished in the state, but by the middle of the 20th century had practically vanished. In

(Photo of otter from Wiki Commons)

1952, the state designated them as a protected species.

Between 1980 and 1983, the Pennsylvania River Otter Reintroduction Project released 21 otters along Pine Creek. Reproduction has been successful.

Mile 4.4 (Mile 13.1) Just south of Stowell Run next to the Rail-Trail is a small section of private land on both sides of the trail. Please respect private boundaries. This also marks the southern boundary of the Leonard Harrison and Colton Point State Parks.

The cabin across the stream here was owned for years by Neil Mack, a retired school teacher from Canton, PA. He was interviewed as a part of an oral history project of the Pine Creek Watershed Rivers Conservation Plan. Excerpts of the 2006 "Voices of Pine Creek" video can be found on the Internet.

Behind the cabin, a trail ascends Burdic Run to the West Rim Trail. Along the way is a beautiful 75-foot waterfall. The waterfall is almost impossible to reach easily though.

High above us, across Pine Creek, snakes the orange-blazed West Rim Trail. The footpath is a sce-

63

nic, long-distance (30 mile) hiking trail that runs adjacent to the west rim of the Pine Creek Gorge. The trail's northern terminus is off the Colton Point Road in Ansonia. The southern terminus is at Rattlesnake Rock, two miles south of Blackwell, PA. One of this trail's best features is the opportunity to view the Gorge from many unobstructed rim-edge vistas. This trail has received multiple accolades and national awards. It was voted by the USA Today newspaper "One of the 50 best trails in the U.S." Outside Magazine named this trail the best hike in Pennsylvania. (1996)

The area of the Rail-Trail south of Stowell Run and north of Tiadaghton is most isolated. It is deep in the bowels of the Canyon with only the creek being prominent. Yet, it is hauntingly beautiful. There are no artificial sounds here. The stillness in Nature is deafening.

Wildlife is visible at times on this section of the trail. Eagles occasionally fly up and down the stream here. Deer may browse close to the trail or in the creek. Birds can be seen and heard. Hawks fly overhead or sit on tree branches.

And sometimes rattlesnakes lie close to the trail or even across the trail.

Rattlesnakes cause terror in hikers and bikers' minds, but there really is little to fear, as long as caution is heeded. They are most often seen sunning themselves in a warm, sunny area.

The yellow phase photo I took at a distance with a telephoto lens as the snake was basking in the late afternoon sunlight.

This might be anyplace the sun is shining near the trail.

Rattlesnakes are generally not aggressive and they avoid humans. Given room, if you see one, the snake will either remain motionless or retreat.

The black phase photo is courtesy of Dave Hughes. I leave the snake seeking to experts like him.

Please, for your safety, do not approach a rattlesnake. Given the isolated nature of the Rail-Trail, emergency help is not readily available, so caution is advised.

Rattlesnakes come in two phase coloring.

A black phase rattlesnake is mottled black; a yellow phase rattlesnake is mottled yellow.

Rattlesnakes "rattle" the modified scales on the end of their tail to make the tell-tale warning sound they are known for.

Rattlesnakes are protected. There are fines associated with harming them.

Some advice:

- Rattlesnakes like summer evenings the best, just as the sun is going down and when it has gone — they are most active nocturnally in the summertime. Use special caution this time of day.

- Rattlesnakes like warm days. Be it any season of the year, even winter, a rattlesnake can venture out in search of the warmth — suitable air temperature for rattlesnakes is from 70° to 90°F (21° to 32°C).

- Most rattlesnakes are not generally sitting about in the open — if they are in the open; they are moving through it much of the time. Rattlesnakes want to avoid contact with predators that can easily spot them in the open, including humans and large animals.

- You will most likely encounter rattlesnakes around rocks, shrubs and brush, or wherever there are nooks for them to hide. However, on sunny days, you might find rattlesnakes warming themselves on warm rocks or on the trail bed gravel.

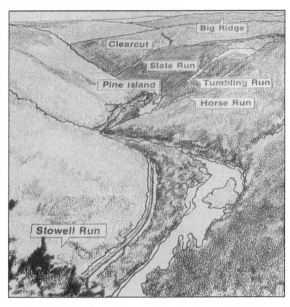

This is part of a sign at Leonard Harrison State Park Overlook.

Mile 4.6 (Mile 13.3) In this vicinity, right at the horse icon signs, a careful search between the trail and creek will turn up a quiet campfire area. It's a good place to take a break. There is no overnight camping here.

Mile 5.3 (Mile 14) Throughout this section of the Trail, there are many small tributaries flowing into the west side of Pine Creek. Burdic Run, Horse Run, Tumbling Run, Little Slate Run, and Ice Break Run are some of several whose names are marked on wooden signs along the Trail.

Many of these small streams flow through steep ravines that have been described as green grottos. Many exist in dimly lit woods, spiked with small rays of sun through parts of the day.

Most of these small tributaries have water only sporadically, mostly in the spring. Most are also practically impassible to humans.

Bradley Wales Overlook, looking north.

In this area, high in the mountains west of here, there are still small stands of rare virgin hemlocks. Also in the same mountains are old Petroglyph paintings done by the First Americans.

Mile 7.3 (Mile 16) South of Ice Break Run, the pines that mark the western ridges of Bradley Wales State Park come into view across the stream. We are now midpoint in the Gorge.

Bradley Wales was the name of a local farmer. Eventually, his lands became Bradley Wales State Park, a tiny speck of restrooms and pavilions with a magnificent view of the Canyon high on the ledges of the mountain.

Bradley Wales State Park can be accessed from the Painter-Leetonia/ West Rim Road, which runs be- *Bringing logs off the mountain on Four Mile Trestle.* tween Colton Point *This trestle was said to be the largest in the Gorge.*

Lookout and Blackwell, PA. Some of the forestry roads in this area are the scene of the annual Susquehannock Trail Road rally.

Arriving at the old railroad bridges at the ghost town of Tiadaghton.

Train crews running the switchbacks of the old Tiadaghton and Fahneystock (pronounced Tie-a-dot-on and Funny-stock) Railroad above Tiadaghton were known to winter over on the Wales farm. The remnants of the switchbacks still remain and are part of a trail that links Bradley Wales State Park and Pine Creek.

The railroad, built by local businessman Creon Farr, zigzagged down the mountain past four switchbacks, on its way 800 foot down to the base of the Gorge where it crossed the creek over a 240-foot bridge.

About the same time Leonard Harrison, a local lumberman, built a sawmill on our side of Pine Creek near Tiadaghton.

Mile 7.40 (Mile 16.1) Tiadaghton, elevation 1150, was the only village built in the Gorge between Ansonia and Blackwell. Tiadaghton was settled because of the railroad and sawmill projects.

The sawmill burned in 1906 and the sawmill operations were then moved to Leetonia on the western side of the Gorge. After that, the town declined rapidly.

The town at one point held about 25 houses, two stores, a hotel, a post office, the sawmill and about 1000 residents, mostly lumberjacks, mill workers, and railroad crews.

Photo courtesy of Tom Gamble. This is the only known photo of the town of Tiadaghton. This picture can also be seen with its labeling description at the Darling Run train station museum.

This is the only place where there may be vehicular traffic on the actual rail-trail. Motorized vehicles are allowed to drive on the side of the trail used by horse traffic. Vehicles drive to the campground, so between the campground and the road leaving the canyon, we may see cars and trucks. Be safe.

This old picture of Tiadaghton was taken in 1902.

In the photo, we can see a New York Central train traveling south. The train is sitting on the bridge we cross near the green camp. The green camp sits on the site of the original post office and general store. A blue dot marks the site in the photo.

Just ahead of the train on the Pine Creek side, the long rectangular building is the train station.

This photo looks to our north back the way we just came. It is taken from the vicinity of where the modern road approaches the rail-trail. Barely in the picture in the far upper left is the old 240-foot trestle bridge that crossed the creek.

The Tiadaghton interpretive panel.

Tom Gamble tells the story of how the road to the top of the mountain was eventually carved out. Locals used dynamite to blast the rock in the vicinity of the first steep incline. Townspeople feared that the rubble of the blast would injure folks, so all of them who were there at the time crawled under the train bridge we just crossed over near the green camp. Sure enough, the rubble flew through the air. A huge boulder was flung on top of the hotel roof and blew a hole right through it and onto the beds on the top floor.

By the 1930's, the Civilian Conservation Corps had torn up the railroad and the wooden trestle bridge that crossed the stream here.

Be sure to stop at the interpretive panel at the campground just ahead of us and read the information about the history of this area and check out the old-time photos.

Mile 7.4 (Mile 16.1) We have arrived at Tiadaghton, the end of this 7.4-mile segment of the Rail–Trail. (According to Strava. The DNCR map says its 7.7 miles)

There is water from a well pump at the campground. There are also latrine bathrooms.

TIADAGHTON TO RATTLESNAKE ROCK

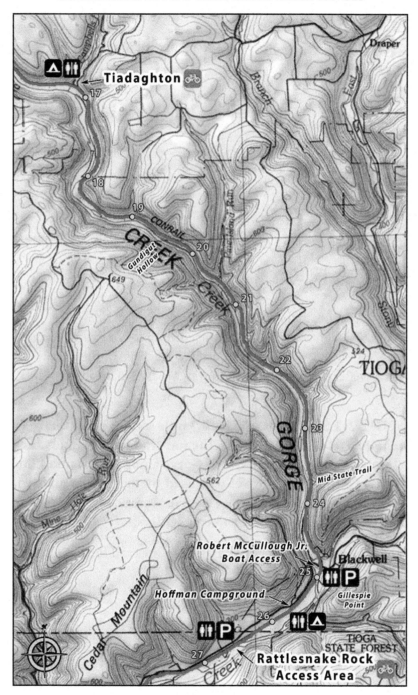

3   TIADAGHTON TO RATTLESNAKE ROCK

This segment of the Pine Creek Rail-Trail is 10.3 miles long. From Tiadaghton to Blackwell, according to Strava, is 8.5 miles (DCNR says 8.3 miles); Rattlesnake Rock is 1.8 miles beyond Blackwell. The nearest food and water is at a small store in Blackwell.

SEGMENT SUMMARY: This 10.3 mile section is another very remote part of the Rail-Trail. The rail-trail follows Pine Creek closely, deep in the Pine Creek Gorge along the original Pine Creek Path, a major travel-way used by the Seneca and Iroquois tribes to oversee other Native American peoples who had been displaced by the pioneer settlers.

There is no easy access to or exit from the trail for the next 8.5 miles of the Trail. (Until Blackwell.)

There is also no food or water along the trail in this section.

We have just passed the site of Tiadaghton, (Pronounced Tie-a-dot'-on) a ghost town deep in the bottom of the Pine Creek Gorge.

The mileages in this book are shown in two ways. The first mileage is always the segment mileage; the overall mileage from the Northern Terminus is the second mileage listed.

Mile 0.0 (Mile 16.1) There are only a few private camps in Tiadaghton now and a nice camping area for hikers/ bikers. (Be sure you get a camping permit if you intend to stay overnight). There is also boat access to Pine Creek at the camping area. During the spring, especially, rafters, canoeists, and kayakers put out here for lunch after a long morning in the Gorge.

The latrine toilet at Tiadaghton campground.

This is a perfect area to rest and relax for a while. Picnic tables are readily available for a quick snack or lunch. (or a nap.)

You may notice that there is a roadway here. The Tiadaghton road returns to civilization and is an emergency access point for the trail and the Pine Creek Gorge. The road, however, is steep and requires four wheel drive and/or a small-sized front-wheel drive vehicle (without a long wheelbase or long wheelbase overhang) to navigate. The last ½ mile is said to be a 20% grade. More than one accident has happened on this steep mountain road and it is impassible certain times of the year.

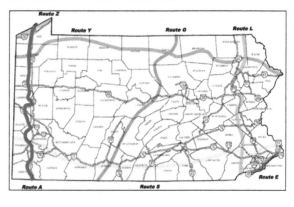

The "G" signs, seen at Tiadaghton, are along the entire Rail-Trail. The G trail is a north-south bike trail that runs through the entire state. The G trail is in pink on the map.

This small buck was quite distressed that I was eating "his" chestnuts along the trail.

Wildlife is often visible at the campground and vicinity.

The last time I was here, a juvenile bald eagle was flying above the trail as I arrived. Once I went to the creek, an adult bald eagle flew just beyond me straight north along the creek bank. Just south of us were three deer grazing in the stream.

While we are at the campground, sharp eyes may spot on the high ledge to the east (our left) a tiny wooden lookout building that hangs perilously off the cliff. Gitchell's Lookout, built in 1938 by the Gitchell family as a private oasis still remains on sentry overlooking this area. It is best seen from the creek south of the campground.

The original railroad was only a single track from Tiadaghton to

The tiny Gitchell's lookout perches on the cliff.

Blackwell, so the accompanying horse trail has disappeared now.

This stone is just south of Tiadaghton. I was told that it is a bore hole for when dynamite was used along the trail.

Mile 1.1 (Mile 17.2) As Pine Creek bends away from us on the right, we will be approaching Good Spring Hollow across the creek. We can't see the tall waterfall from the trail, but it is close by.

As the trail straightens and starts to bend back to the left, there is a nondescript path to the right. It very shortly arrives at the water and a small campfire area.

This rest area off the trail, but on Pine Creek, has the perfect view of Falling Spring waterfall. Notice the dark green color of Pine Creek the day this photo was taken in the spring.

Again, please respect the rules here. There is no camping overnight along the rail-trail except at designated areas. This is not a designated area.

In the Spring especially, Falling Spring waterfall has a good flow of water. It is said to be the tallest waterfall in the Gorge. If it has been a dry season, more than likely, it will be dry, though. In the winter, it is often a massive, dangerous, wall of ice.

Mile 2.6 (Mile 18.7, DNCR mile marker 19) This is a nice bench to rest on. I've slept here before.

Mile 2.9 (Mile 19) We may see remnants of "slide fences" along the way north of Blackwell. These wood-walled embankments were built by the railroad to help prevent landslides onto the tracks.

If a slide hit the fence, it would cause a signal to display red to stop all trains. Depending on the severity of the slide, the train was allowed to proceed cautiously or the train had to wait for a crew to be dispatched to remove the debris.

For many years, the railroad had pretty frequent landslides in

this area, which would shut down the train schedule, sometimes for weeks or months at a time.

Many of the paths off the rail-trail, in early May, have abundant and sometimes rare wildflowers. Only once a year, these precious plants appear.

The photo on the left is a rare Lady Slipper. The trillium on the right is only one trillium in a sea of trilliums just off the rail-trail in this vicinity.

Mile 3.2 (Mile 19.3) High above and on our side of the Gorge is Red Ledge Ridge, elevation 1785. In the 1940's, there were two private lookouts here. Both were, for a time, open to the public for events.

Stories abound of the dances and church meetings that were held here. All of these old-time lookouts are now on private property and are closed off to the public.

Mile 3.3 (Mile 19.4) On the West side of the Canyon is Gundigut Hollow. The word "Gundigut", as in Gundigut Hollow, is a strange one. According to local legend, there was an island in the stream in this vicinity that blocked the logs as they floated downstream. The small opening in the channel was called the "gut" and logs were supposed to be threaded through the tiny channel so that they didn't get hung up there. Old-time German loggers

Riding along below Falling Spring with Pine Creek on our right.

would shout "Gun di Gut!" as they fought to get the logs through this section of the stream. The term stuck.

The forest here changes from mixed hardwoods to an oak forest. High on the mountain are a few Native American chestnut trees that have survived the chestnut blight over the years. These few trees with a genetic resistance to the blight are reminders of what was once a common tree in the woods here. (Dillon)

An understory plant in the entire Gorge is the Pennsylvania state flower, the Mountain Laurel.

This hardy evergreen can grow several stories tall under the right conditions.

In early to mid-June, beautiful rhododendron-like flowers appear. Each individual flower is white, star-shaped with pink inserts.

Mountain Laurel in June.

Mile 3.5 (Mile 19.6) Just past the huge rock on the right side of the trail, is a former landslide area. There are lots of rocks for rattlesnakes to bask among here. Use caution. This entire area, from here south to Blackwell is known for being populated with rattlesnakes. It is possible you will see one on the trail. Please do not approach it. (See pages 64-65 for information on these snakes)

Mile 4.1 (Mile 20.2) We pass Pine Island Run here. Pine Island Run is classified as a wild trout stream. In the spring, it also hosts a nice waterfall. Between us and the creek here is the old site of a log landing for the Tiadaghton sawmill. Looking up, we will see Pine Island Ledge, along the eastern upper reaches of the mountain top on our side of the creek. This bluff is as magnificent as Barbour Rocks, but is on private property.

Mile 5.3 (Mile 21.4) We pass Benjamin Hollow and Railroad marker L-128 in this area. This stream has a 50-foot waterfall high along the path. It probably will be dry if you are riding anytime but spring, although the 2015 summer season saw good flow in these waterfalls into mid-July.

There is always something to see even on the most remote sections of the trail. There is a bald eagle nest in this vicinity.

In this area, in January 1899, Passenger train #6 wrecked when a tree, uprooted by the wind, came tearing down the mountainside, went under the engine tender, and knocked the train off the tracks. No one was injured. The Wellsboro Agitator newspaper reported that the railroad's "clean record of not killing any passengers" still stood.

Mile 6 (Mile 22.1) At Water Tank Run, steam engines used to stop to fill their boilers up with water. There was a dam here in the hollow on our side of the creek, and wooden pipes were used to bring the water to a tank near the tracks. There are a few remnants of the old rotted wooden pipes, high in the woods here. The pipes were made of white oak, because the pores of this wood are filled with a resinous substance that allows the wood to hold liquids. (Dillon)

The bridge over Water Tank Hollow.

These photos were taken in mid-April which is about the earliest I venture onto the trail. Many years, there is ice and snow on the trail until then. Even this day, there was snow along the trail in shady spots.

There are old fire pits in the woods near Clay Mine Run where bricks were made for a time. Clay was readily available here and so it was used to make Fire Clay, a heat resistant brick.

Standing on the bridge at Water Tank Hollow in April.

The enterprise didn't last long because of technical difficulties. Clay doesn't slide easily in troughs. It was all hard work here in the 1800 and 1900's.

An old photo of workers at a local clay mine.

Early in the 1800's, the Pine Creek Gorge was home to a massive elk herd. Philip Tome, author of "Pioneer Life: 30 Years a Hunter" describes seeing elk throughout the Pine Creek Gorge. Most of the year, they stayed in the mountains surrounding Pine Creek, but during the summer months they often stayed at the creek where fresh moss and new greens were abundant.

There are fascinating stories about Tome's exploits, many of them captured in his Pioneer Life book.

There is a tiered waterfall high up in Water Tank Hollow.

An illustration from "Pioneer Life: 30 Years a Hunter".

Tome was originally from Slate Run, further south on the rail-trail. He learned to hunt from skilled frontiersmen and from members of the Seneca Indian tribe. He eventually became friends with Chief Cornplanter, who lived further west of here. He was an interpreter and guide in his later years.

He says that Chief Cornplanter bet him that he could not capture an elk alive. Members of his tribe had tried and were unsuccessful. So Tome set out to prove that he could. He came to Pine Creek where several large bull elk had been spotted. They pursued the elk with hounds (which was legal at the time) for miles and the elk eventually climbed up on a large rock. Tome and his companion then climbed a tree, lassoed the elk around the antlers and tied the elk to a horse.

According to Tome, the elk was 16 hands, 5' 4" - with antlers 6 ft. long and 11 points on each side. The elk was valued at $1,000. Tome and several friends were able to keep the elk under control and wrestle him onto a raft. They floated the Allegheny River to our north to Olean, NY where the public paid $12.00 a person to see the large animal.

Tome's stories give a fun account of what life was like in the mid to late 1800's for frontiersmen. I suspect some of his accounts are more than a little exaggerated though.

There is a wild elk herd now in Elk County, a few hours west of the rail-trail. The herd numbers between 800 and 900 elk. (Pennsylvania Game News)

There is some discussion that as the elk proliferate, they are moving slowly into this area again. Local legend says that there may be elk living in the western reaches of the Gorge. It makes a nice story, whether it is true or not.

There is a photograph on display at the Darling Run train station of an elk at Fourmile Run that was taken by a local resident in 1998.

Mile 6.7 (Mile 22.8) We have passed another eagle's nest, so eagle sightings across the stream are more likely here. You may see a white dot high on the mountain side. That will be the eagle's white head.

More frequently seen in the Canyon are turkey vultures riding the air currents high above us. The large black birds may be mistaken for eagles from a distance. They have a bright red head and are rather ugly.

Mile 7.2 (Mile 23.3) The orange-blazed Mid State Trail intersects the rail-trail at Stone Quarry Run. The Mid State Trail follows along the rail-trail to the village of Blackwell. The Mid State Trail is an almost 324-mile trail that runs from the New York State Border in Tioga County to the Pennsylvania- Maryland border. It is a part of the larger Eastern Trail System, a trail that parallels the Appalachian Trail along the entire eastern seaboard.

The Mid State Trail ascends Gillespie Point at Blackwell and continues on its north- south route.

The sign where the Mid State Trail joins with the rail-trail.

Across from the Stone Quarry Run and across the creek, we may see a small campsite along the Bohen Run Trail, close to Pine Creek. This trail leaves Blackwell and follows the stream north to this point where it turns to follow Bohen Hollow up the side of the mountain. The Bohen Trail connects to the West Rim Trail close to the top of Big Ridge.

Old Stone Quarry Point, at the top of Stone Quarry Run is named for the quarry located here. The sandstone used in the building of the Tioga County Courthouse in Wellsboro reportedly came from this quarry.

Mile 7.5 (Mile 23.6) We may see the waterfalls at Jerry Run across the stream in the spring.

It is possible that there may be a "hatch" on Pine Creek when we ride through here. North of Blackwell is a prime area for being bombarded by flying nymphs.

These aquatic insects start their lives in the waters of Pine Creek. Mayflies and caddis flies are plentiful at certain times of the year. Their presence signals that the waters here are pure and that the stream quality is excellent.

At different times in the spring, within minutes hundreds of thousands of these insects break from their skins or cocoons and emerge. These flies float to the surface of the stream where they sit to dry their wings. At this point, trout in the stream often come to the surface to snatch these waiting flies. Survivors fly into the air, mate within hours, drop their eggs, and die.

Pine Creek Outfitter watercrafts pass by Jerry Run falls on Pine Creek in April.

Fly fishermen often time their fishing excursions according to the "hatch" and match their artificial flies to the hatch of the day or week.

Mayflies are especially susceptible to water pollution and Babb Creek's water which enters Pine Creek at Blackwell, just .7 miles south of here has historically been polluted by mine acid from mines to the east of this area. The hatch diminishes south of Blackwell for several miles for this reason. In the Slate Run area, to the south, the hatch returns and fishing is superb.

Babb's Creek has undergone ongoing reclamation over several decades to improve the water quality in this stream.

Mile 8.4 (Mile 24.5) The village of Blackwell, elevation 875, lies along Pine Creek. Blackwell was settled first in 1811 by Enoch Blackwell, Sr.

Blackwells, as it was known on the early maps,

(The original picture is in the Darling Run station museum)

became a busy center for railroading and lumbering over the years. There are many remnants here of the railroad days.

On the north side of Blackwell, off Blackwell Square, is the original Blackwell church.

Then and now pictures are eerily similar.

The Methodist Episcopal Church of Blackwells was erected in 1892. Here it is now.

The old Railroad House was built in 1884 and later became the Barton House hotel building that still stands next to the rail-trail.

(This old photo of Blackwell is courtesy of David Ira Kagan, Pine Creek Villages, Arcadia Publishing)

The Old Barton House Hotel now.

It can barely be seen in the background in the picture on the previous page. It was originally a boarding home for railway workers. It also housed a general store and post office for a time.

Blackwell is home to a few year-round residents and some seasonal camps. The store here is a fine place to stop for snacks and ice cream. It's just off the trail as the trail crosses Route 414. It is the only place we can stock up on bottled water as we head south.

To our right, at Blackwell is the **Robert McCullough, Jr. boating and fishing access point**. It is not technically a biking access point. The biking access point and parking area is 1.8 miles further south at Rattlesnake Rock. (See page 190 for driving directions) If its not busy, bikers sometimes use this lot for access to the trail.

There is a river gauge at the parking area. Pine Creek is only suitable for shallow draft, lightweight boats, canoes, kayaks, or inflatables. April and May are known as the best months for boating here. By summer, the water level has dropped too low for boating without scraping. A launch permit and boat registration are required.

The No Scrape Water depth for Pine Creek is 3 feet between Ansonia and Cammal, 2.8 feet from Cammal to Waterville, and 2.5 feet from Waterville to Jersey Shore.

The Robert McCullough, Jr. Boating and Fishing Access Area.

There is a public-access free telephone at the Blackwell parking area. It can be used to call 911 or to make local calls. This is the only phone service available, since there is no cell phone service in this entire area.

There are also latrine restrooms, picnic tables, and a water pump here.

Stop to read the interpretive panel for information about the Pine Creek Gorge.

One morning, I was at the Blackwell parking lot as hunters came out of

There are a local call phone and comfort stations at the Mc-Cullough Access Area.

The old railroad bridge over Pine Creek as seen from the McCullough access area.

the woods. One of them looked at the railroad bridge downstream and commented that it looked like a dog was crossing the stream. Upon closer inspection, it was a black bear. Of all my trips on the Rail-Trail, this is the only bear I have seen. (Other than the massive 630 pound mounted bear inside the Hotel Manor in Slate Run.)

Gillespie Point is just southwest of the village of Blackwell. The vista from Gillespie Point is said to be one of the best vistas in the Gorge. The Mid State Trail travels past Gillespie Point. The mountain's Matterhorn shape is not visible here, but will be visible further south.

The merging of Pine Creek and Babb's Creek at Blackwell was known to the First Americans as the Second Fork of the Pine Creek Path.

An archaeological dig near the railroad grade here found artifacts that indicated that Native Americans camped at this location seasonally about 1000 years ago. (Dillon)

Mile 8.5 (Mile 24.6) There is a rise in the trail from the roadway to the rail bridge over Pine Creek here. Originally there was a railroad bridge over the roadway, but it has been removed.

A cut for the trail just south of Blackwell.

This is perhaps the second "hill" of three on the rail-trail.

The trail crosses an intact railroad bridge just south of the parking access area. It has a wooden bed and is rough--very noisy.

The 1.8 mile section between Blackwell and Rattlesnake Rock is the longest straight section of the former railroad. From Blackwell to Cedar Run there is the slightest downhill grade.

There is a good example here of one of the deep and long cuts that were made in the land to keep the grade on the railroad bed mostly level. These cuts were made entirely with pick, shovel, a little dynamite, and a wheelbarrow for the most part.

Mile 9.2 (Mile 25.3) Hoffman Campground is 2/3 of a mile south of Blackwell.

There is a turnoff from the trail to the campground. Note the sign. The campground is down the hill.

There are shade trees, picnic tables, campsites, a small pavilion, and a water pump at the campground. Pine Creek is easily accessible because of the low banks here. This campsite is for primitive camping only. A camping permit is required.

Hoffman Campground is the closest primitive campground to

Hoffman Campground. The well is on the right; the latrine restroom is in the middle. Beyond the large grassy area is Pine Creek.

the ½ way mark on the trail and makes for a convenient, overnight stop when doing the whole trail. It is 26 miles to the northern terminus and 36 miles to the southern terminus from here.

There is no access to this campground by vehicle. It's only entrance is via the rail-trail.

The water here is like that at most well pumps. It has a metallic taste.

Mile 10.3 (Mile 26.4) Rattlesnake Rock access area. We have arrived at latrine restrooms and a parking lot used to access the rail-trail as well as the West Rim hiking trail, across the highway here. There is a short steep uphill path to our right to the parking lot.

The exit to the Rattlesnake Rock parking area, up the hill on the right.

RATTLESNAKE ROCK TO SLATE RUN

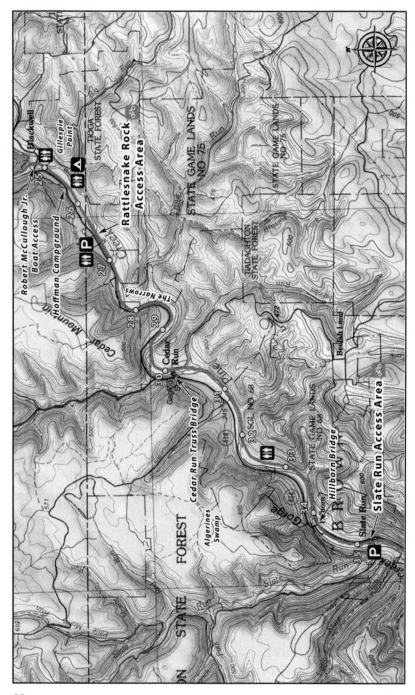

RATTLESNAKE ROCK TO SLATE RUN

4

The Pine Creek Rail-Trail continues at Rattlesnake Rock, 1.8 miles south of Blackwell, PA. There is a large access area here, including latrine restrooms and large parking areas. (See page 190 for details)

SEGMENT SUMMARY: This section of the trail is 8.8 miles long. It follows the highway for a bit before setting out along a wide valley. We skirt the Cedar Run Narrows before we cruise through the magnificent steel truss bridge at Cedar Run. A short distance south and we arrive at the tiny pictur-esque town of Cedar Run. South of town, we bicycle a long section of canopied, shaded trail as Pine Creek becomes wider and more placid. Past the comfort station, we soon cross the highway and follow parallel to it to the town of Slate Run, known for its restau-

93

rant, general store, and fantastic catch and release fly fishing.

The Rail-Trail at Rattlesnake Rock is behind and below the parking lot and restrooms. There is a short path, past the bathrooms that connects the two.

There is boater access here just south of the parking lot, but no camping.

There is a phone at the main parking area that can be used to call 911 or to make local calls.

We have now entered into Lycoming County.

The mileages in this book are shown in two ways. The first mileage is always the segment mileage; the overall mileage from the Northern Terminus is the second mileage listed.

Mile 0.0 (Mile 26.4) Philip Tome, author of "Pioneer Life, Thirty years a Hunter" described Rattlesnake Rock in 1854.

> *"Lying in the river, about twelve feet from the nearest shore was a rock about forty feet long by fifteen wide, called Rattlesnake Rock. On this, the snakes would often lie in piles. On the opposite side of the river was another seventy feet long and twenty wide, on which could often be seen forty snakes at a time".*

Tome also tells the story of two men who in 1794 had taken a trip north on Pine Creek to check on the elk population and to see if there were First Nation tribes here. They found rattlesnakes all along the creek, but here they found the snakes so numerous that they ended up anchoring their canoe off shore to keep the snakes from entering it while on shore. The first night they built a fire at their campsite, but when the snakes arrived before morning,

Standing on Rattlesnake Rock in Pine Creek.

they decided it would be safer to sleep in the canoe in the creek. So they did. The gnats were so bad that they rigged a way to build a fire on top of their canoe to use as a smudge fire. The explorers moved on quickly, but the stories remained.

Tome's fascinating book has many early accounts of frontier life on Pine Creek. Whether his stories are exaggerated or not, is up to the reader's imagination.

In many trips to this set of rocks, I have not seen rattlesnakes here. There are ample blueberries at the rocks, though and folklore says that where there are blueberries, there are rattlesnakes. Please use caution and do not put your hands or feet anywhere you cannot see first.

This is a favorite swimming and fishing hole, so sometimes this area is a hub of activity in the spring and summer. To find the rocks, take the footpath to the left (looking south) from the intersection of the path up to the parking area. You will wind your way through a small, sparse woods until you get to the rocks.

The Rail-Trail follows RT. 414 through this section. The highway will often be just to the west of and very close to the trail.

Rattlesnake Rock on a hot summer afternoon.

Just south of Rattlesnake Rock, the rail-trail will cut through a tunnel of sycamore trees. These trees are unusual looking. They are light gray with bark that flakes off in large pieces. There will often be bark lying on the rail-trail.

Mile 0.5 (Mile 26.9) Lloyd Run enters across the highway from the trail. Lloyd Run is named after Thomas Lloyd, who came with the Blackwell family to settle in the "Eden on Pine Creek"; a proposed Utopian community led by Jon Hay, a Presbyterian minister. Instead of finding "Eden", pioneers found a thick hemlock and pine forest. Most of the new residents left shortly, but the Blackwells and the Lloyds stayed on. In the late 1880's there was a small village here. (Dillon)

Mile 0.6 (Mile 27) Woodhouse Run enters to the west of the trail, just across the highway. The building in the photo on the next page was a former "section" station for the railroad. The sign says 1881. This is one of the few sections of the trail where the highway is close to the rail-trail.

Here is an old photo of a train here. We are looking north in this picture, back the way we just came.

(Photo courtesy of Tim and Emily Losinger. Emily's family homestead was here.)

In February 1897, according to the Wellsboro Agitator newspaper, Passenger train #1 was barreling down the tracks here and ran right into a tree on the tracks. The engine was thrown off the track and the whole train rolled down the embankment into Pine Creek. No one was hurt. In fact, for the entire history of the railroad, they prided themselves on not having killed any of their passengers. And that's the words they used.

Mile 0.9 (Mile 27.3) Three-tenths of a mile past the Woodhouse building we will start through a wide valley. Ahead of us is Bull Run Point on the mountain and the roadway "Narrows". Look for the guardrails on the mountainside. The road will bear away from us now. As we pedal along, we glance behind us occasionally. Right past the "Falling Rock" sign, the Matterhorn shaped mountain at Blackwell called

Woodhouse in the spring.

97

This photo was taken from the highway above but shows Gillespie Point clearly.

Gillespie Point will come into view behind us. It's the one with the pointy peak.

Mile 1.8 (Mile 28.2) The Narrows is a section of roadway that is high above us here. Pine Creek makes a big horseshoe turn between mile 28 and 29.

A view of the Narrows from the roadway.

Over the years, the roadway has been unstable, high on the mountainside.

It has traditionally been one lane, with pull-offs along the way. If two cars meet, one must back up to the nearest pull-off so that they can pass. Several years ago, the Pennsylvania Department of Transportation did renovations to the roadway here after a major slide. During that time, the road was diverted onto the Rail-Trail for a period of time. Now that the roadway

has been repaired, the Rail-Trail is isolated to traffic in this area again.

If you look carefully, you may see the guard rails high above the Rail- Trail in the picture I took from the trail.

I found this evidence of a bear's appearance on the trail, right here.

Looking back towards Blackwell this area is one of the most picturesque spots on the rail-trail, in my opinion.

This 1920's photo was taken at almost the same spot as the photo on the next page that I took this year.

We may notice a railroad sign at the bottom of the narrows that reads "ABL". It faces north, so you will have to turn around to see it.

(Photo courtesy of Mike Spencer).

The letters stand for "Approach Block Limit". A railroad is divided into "block sections" that are meant to keep trains spread out. An engineer may not proceed past his "block" without permission.

On occasion, a train would have to wait here until the all clear was given.

Mile 2.1 (Mile 28.5) This is such a nice old barn along the highway. Notice the window in the second story. It's a little hard to see from the rail-trail. Look to your right, across the highway.

Mile 2.4 (Mile 28.8) Across the highway, headed south, look carefully. We will see Pine Creek's own version of the old fash-

ioned Burma Shave signs. These signs remind folks to care for the area so that others may enjoy it in the future.

Mile 2.7 (Mile 29.1) The beautiful old three span Warren type through-truss railroad bridge north of Cedar Run is one of the highlights of the Rail-Trail. It is picture perfect in all seasons and at all times of the day.

The magnificent old bridge rests just north of Pettecoat Junction, a large campground along the stream bank. There are often visitors on the bridge. You may also see kayakers in the area.

The flat area along the water where the campground now is built was the original location of the massive steam sawmill of John S. Tomb in the 1880's.

This photo was taken from Pettecoat Junction and is looking north, back the way we have come. Please respect their private property and do not trespass.

Mile 3.2 (Mile 29.6) The old stone marker L-136 is in this area. It signifies that we are 136 miles from the northern headquarters of the New York Central Railroad in Lyons, NY. The entire railroad had mile markers showing the distance to the northern headquarters of the railroad. These markers are quite accurate.

The streams of Cedar Run and Slate Run were significant to the development of the lumber industry here in the 1800s. But the abundance of fish and game were as strong a draw for the early settlers as logging.

Jacob Lamb is believed to be the first to settle in the area. Lamb hosted church services in his home as early as 1805. Cedar Run

had sawmills as early as 1819, and a post office after 1853.

At the height of its prosperity in 1890, Cedar Run had a population of 885.

In the 1880s and most of the 1890s, a daily stagecoach carried passengers and freight between the nearby lumbering villages of Leetonia and Cedar Run and its station on the railroad line along Pine Creek.

These photos are of the summer and winter stage-coaches. Photos courtesy of Thomas T. Taber, III. First photo taken by Nelson A. Caulkins.

The Cedar Run Inn and the Cedar Run General Store opened in the early 1890s and remain open. A nearby Young Men's Christian Association (YMCA) summer camp (Camp Cedar Pines) for boys and girls brought visitors to the area between 1920 and 1946.

Mile 3.4 (Mile 29.8) Cedar Run now has around 30 some households, 2/3rd of which are seasonal camps. It is the perfect place to pull off the trail and sit awhile.

Looking from the trail towards Pine Creek. Ice cream on the left. Rooms and dinner on the right.

There is only one main street in Cedar Run flanked by the Cedar Run General Store and the Cedar Run Inn.

The Cedar Run Inn is known for its world-class food and comfortable guest rooms.

And the General Store is the perfect place for an ice cream cone, sandwich, or souvenirs. Stop in to either place to say hello. Both welcome visitors.

Be sure to exit the trail and explore Cedar Run. Past the two main buildings in town, the main street turns left and crosses over Pine Creek.

The small road to Pettecoat Junction, the campground, goes to the right just before the stream.

My bike sits in front of the Cedar Run store.

Along the small road are benches and a perfect view of Pine Creek and the mountainside. We may glimpse folks basking at the local swimming hole just up the creek.

There is an eagle nest on the mountain also, so we may see an eagle anywhere in this area. Often they sit just off the modern bridge across the stream.

One day I was standing on the bridge and a juvenile bald eagle came loudly screaming up the stream bed. He passed between

The Cedar Run bridge as seen from a bench along Pine Creek.

me on the bridge and the kayakers below on the stream. We were both awed!

The old red Methodist Episcopal Church at the bridge was built in 1897. It is now privately owned.

This sign at the bridge humorously points out distances to a variety of locations.

Pine Creek is 150 feet away. Disney World is 922 miles away. Singapore is 7663 miles away.

There are several camp rentals along the rail-trail and side roads in this vicinity.

There is also a large modern campground just north of town called Pettecoat Junction. Since Cedar Run lies closest to the ½ way mark on the rail-trail, it's a great place to stay when riding the whole trail.

Cedar Run is another town steeped in railroad history. At one time, Cedar Run had a clock station and a water tower near Jacobs Run.

Pusher steam locomotives sometimes were deployed from here to above Blackwell because of the grade when headed north. Passenger and freight trains shared the rails through the canyon on a daily basis. Passenger trains ran at least twice a day, in the morning and then again in the evening. Three to four freight trains also passed through here on a daily basis.

Old-timers remember that the whistle on the passenger train was different than the freight trains and that the passenger train was the one that carried the mail. When they heard the whistle blow, the townsfolk would gather at the station to greet visitors and wave to the passengers. They would then wait for the mail to be sorted at the nearby post office. Train arrival was a high point of the day.

This old stone sign just north of town gives the signal to the engineer to blow the whistle.

Mile 3.6 (Mile 30) Just south of Cedar Run, there is a fleeting cell phone signal, good enough for text messages. The signal lasts until around DCNR Mile Marker 31.

Through this section of the rail-trail, we travel over several small railroad bridges that cross over Jacobs Run, Elk Run, and Hilborn Run. Feel the cool breeze coming out of the glens as we pass over the bridges.

The Cedar Run Inn and the train station with semaphore, (Photo courtesy of David Ira Kagan, Pine Creek Villages, Arcadia Publishing)

The first stream, Jacob's Run was the site of an old water tower.

Look carefully here for the pier on the right and the interesting rock art with the rock balanced on top.

A tunnel of trees just south of Cedar Run at Jacobs Run.

For the next mile and a half, there are benches and pull offs poised along the trail, at ½ mile increments.

When we pass the little stone dam across Pine Creek about ½ mile south of Cedar Run, listen for the sound of water running. A tiny grotto and falls is to our left, below us. It is posted as private property, so please do not go exploring.

107

A fly fisherman in Pine Creek near Old Stone mileage Marker L-137.

Mile 4.6 (Mile 31) We are now ½ way through our 62 mile trip on the Pine Creek Rail-Trail.

Across the stream, we pass the Gamble Run boating access area, south of Cedar Run. There are very limited resources here.

All through this area the fishing is excellent.

One day I rode past this fisherman and struck up a conversation. He told me that I should look out for an eagle that had just been in the area. He laughed and commented that eagles sometimes fight the fishermen for trout the fishermen catch. Eagles always are opportunists!

Yes, this is in Pine Creek.

As I took the following picture one day, I heard an eagle's call so I started looking for him. A juvenile bald eagle was sitting in one of the trees across the stream. July is an especially good time to hear eagles call-ing.

The newly fledged eaglets (which are the size of an adult

Looking across Pine Creek below Gamble Run.

bird, but black) don't hunt yet. So they sit on a branch and call to their parents to bring food to them. We may even see an adult swoop up with a fish in his/her talon and give it to the eaglet.

This section of the trail always seems to be a hotbed for wildlife. Many users of the trail report seeing deer and bear, especially here.

The deer in this photo are close to this biker on the trail.

And one day, this bear cub came across Pine Creek and onto the

(Deer photo courtesy of Nicole Hewitt)

(Bear photo courtesy of Bob Burns)

trail just north of the Hilborn Fields Comfort Station. Both the runner and the bear were surprised.

109

The Hilborn Fields Comfort Station as we ride south.

You may notice that this entire section of the trail from Cedar Run to the highway north of Slate Run is shaded and tree canopied.

When I ride here in the morning, it's shaded; when I ride back through in the afternoon, it's still shaded.

The gravel is a little loose on the trail from Cedar Run south, so be careful as you gaze across Pine Creek.

I am also reminded of the rhythm of the "Snap, Crackle, and Pop" of my wheels on the limestone gravel, usually the only sounds of the ride through here.

Mile 6.1 (Mile 32.5) Another mile and a half south on the trail is the Hilborn Field Comfort Station. These pit toilet restrooms are maintained by DCNR. The highway is far across these fields to our right, along the mountain.

These rattlesnake information signs are dispersed along the trail.

Loggers in the 1800's.

To the west, across the stream is the 84-acre Algerine Swamp Natural Area. It is part of the Tiadaghton State Forest. Two uncommon trees inhabit this area: black spruce and balsam fir. This area, high on the mountain is a natural bog. The Algerine Swamp had a rather notorious history during the logging era.

This story from Chuck Dillon follows:

The Algerines were Algerian pirates in the early 1800's, whom the U.S. Marines defeated in 1815. The term was used for anyone who seized goods or people as hostage for monetary payment and was applied to the unethical loggers of the time.

When lumber was floated down Pine Creek, a stamp was made on the butt of each log to identify who owned it. However, if a log washed ashore, and if no one was there to see, opportunists sawed off the butt of the log where the stamp as made and put their own stamp on the new butt.

The "Algerine" outlaws made their homes in the Algerine Swamps. According to legend, in their home area, high on the mountain, these pirates were as "invisible" as the stealthy deer that now live in the swamp.

Mile 7.7 (Mile 34.1) We see houses on our right just before we arrive at Route 414, north of Slate Run. Gaze to your right, as you come towards the yellow gate before the highway.

Riding north to Cedar Run on a gorgeous July afternoon.

You may want to exit the trail here and ride over to the bridge (towards your right, headed south).

The 202-foot, single span bridge is a "Quintangular" lattice through truss bridge built by the Berlin Bridge Company in 1890. It was rehabilitated in 1950. It is on the National Register of Historic Places.

If you cross the highway without visiting the bridge, be very careful. Visibility is limited at the crossing.

Immediately after the highway, crossing look to our left for an old railroad sign.

Mile 7.9 (Mile 34.3) The highway follows just above us and to the left of us from here to the village of Slate Run, just a mile away. There will be open fields to our right now and Pine Creek

will be beyond the fields. Some of these fields were the site of the large hemlock sawmill owned by J.B. Weed and Company.

Mile 8.8 (Mile 35.2) Slate Run, elevation 715, awaits. At this point, it feels like we have returned to civilization. Once the woods open up, the Rail-Trail parallels Route 414 all the way to Slate Run. Camps and resident homes line the creek.

From here south, the valley is much wider and there are many signs that remind us that it is the 21st century.

We will pass several houses and yellow gate crossings over their driveways.

North of this point, it is easy to find moments and sometimes hours that feel like it could be the 19th century as easily as the 21st.

It's time to pause and relax at water's edge in Slate Run. Explore the Hotel Manor across Pine Creek for nourishment or a hotel room and/or the Slate Run Store and Tackle Shop right on the highway for food, bike supplies and rentals, fishing equipment, and souvenirs.

Wolfe's General Store sits on the highway. There is a path from the trail at the back of the building to the store.

There is an awesome 630 pound black bear inside the Hotel Manor.

Hotel Manor, as seen from the highway bridge at Slate Run.

SLATE RUN TO CAMMAL

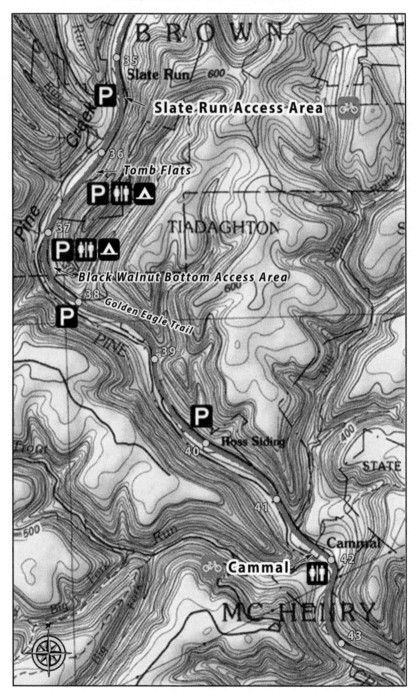

SLATE RUN TO CAMMAL · 5

SEGMENT SUMMARY: The Pine Creek Rail-Trail continues on this 6.6-mile section of the north-south pathway through the Pine Creek Valley. It's a peaceful trip alongside Pine Creek past two campgrounds, a pioneer cemetery, trailheads to well-rated trail loops, and plenty of opportunities to see wildlife. The trail is often close to the major highway that runs through this area. There are highway crossings on this section of the trail.

At Slate Run, there is a large trail access area and parking lot. There are no restrooms here, though. There are restrooms a mile south at Tombs Flats. (See page 192 for details.)

The Rail-Trail is above the parking lot that is near the creek. The access area and the fields just north of it are the original locations for the huge hemlock sawmill of James B. Weed that operated in the late 1800's and early 1900's during the lumber boom days.

This is a pleasant place to rest and watch the activity in the creek. The stream widens and there are good views to the north and south along the water. This is a good place to spot eagles.

(Picture Courtesy of Slate Run Tackle Shop)

Often there are fly fishermen here as there are several fishing holes in this section of the stream. The waters are crystal clear and have very little sediment. Pine Creek is also fairly easy to wade, even though it is wide across. Fly fishermen are easily recognized by their hip waders and fly rods with long lines that they flick back and forth onto the surface of the water.

The stream named Slate Run enters into Pine Creek here. This stream is listed by the state as a Class A wild trout stream. It is full of brook and brown trout and is managed under restrictive harvest regulations.

The regulations require that those fishing at Slate Run must use fly fishing tackle, including flies and barbless hooks. Any fish caught here must be immediately released back into the stream.

Cedar Run and Jacobs Run, near Cedar Run village, and Four-mile Run, near the Turkey Path are also Class A trout streams. Pine Island Run, north of Blackwell, is designated Wilderness Trout Waters. We may see signs along the Rail- Trail that describe this area as "Delayed Harvest Artificial Lure" Only. These restrictions are for the 2.8 miles between Slate Run and Bonnell Run at the Clark Farm/Utceter access area. Under these regulations, fishermen may keep a daily limit of trout during certain times of the year.

Two noticeable points of interest in Slate Run have to do with nourishment.

The bridge behind Hotel Manor. (Picture courtesy of Hotel Manor)

The first, the Hotel Manor sits across the creek from the trail, but is easily accessed across the modern bridge. Dining is available indoors as well as outdoors on the deck overlooking Pine Creek. Overnight accommodations are also available here.

There is a plaque honoring Jacob Tomb outside the Hotel Manor.

There is weak cell phone service here. Ask nicely and the Hotel Manor staff may let you connect to their hotel wi-fi.

The Black Forest Trail starts and finishes in the Tiadaghton State Forest behind Hotel Manor.

The Black Forest Trail is a 42-mile loop trail named after the dense, dark, virgin hemlock stands that originally stood here. Behind the hotel is a pretty 100-foot steel truss bridge that DNCR just set across Slate Run and a connecting path to the Black Forest Trail.

The second place to get nourishment is Wolfe's General Store, right on RT. 414. They have made-to-order deli sandwiches, a general grocery store, and ice cream. There is a little path from the Rail-Trail around the building to the front door.

Wolfe's General Store and the Slate Run Tackle Shop are built just behind where the original Slate Run railroad depot was located.

There is spotty cell phone service on the front porch at Wolfe's store and a reasonable signal inside the store.

The rear section of Wolfe's. Those are all "flies" for fly-fishing in those cases.

In the back of the general store is a tackle shop that specializes in fly fishing information and equipment.

It is interesting to stop in and look at the artificial flies for sale. These flies are hand "tied" and resemble real insects that hatch along Pine Creek. They are used by fishermen as lures. Many consider fly tying an art. Some hand-made flies sell for a dollar or so. Others may be sold for many times that amount, depending on how exotic the materials that were used are.

(Green caddis artificial lure on left and real insect, on right, a popular hatch in late April)

Photo of Slate Run, courtesy of David Ira Kagan, Pine Creek Villages, Arcadia Publishing

Jacob Tome (also spelled Tomb) is credited with being the first settler at the mouth of Slate Run. In 1791, he moved his family from Milton up the creek in ten canoes and reached his point of destination in November of that year. Jacob Tomb was an active and enterprising man. He erected gristmills and sawmills in 1796.

Benjamin, son of Jacob and Jane Tomb, was born in the month of March, 1795, at the mouth of Slate run, and he is believed to have been the first non-native child born that far up Pine creek.

Another of Jacob's sons, Philip Tomb (he used the Tome spelling) wrote an account of his life as a frontiersman. The book "Pioneer Life: Thirty Years a Hunter" is a delight to read for its entertaining stories of hunting in the Pine Creek area. (See page 81-82 for more about Philip Tome.)

Slate Run was a busy place during the lumbering era. The main line railroad existed on the right of way for the Rail-Trail, but there were other narrow gauge railroads coming into the village from the mountains to the north and west.

The mileages in this book are shown in two ways. The first mileage is always the segment mileage; the overall mileage from the Northern Terminus is the second mileage listed.

South of Slate Run, a fly fisherman fishes on the far side of Pine Creek.

Mile 0.0 (Mile 35.2) The Pine Creek Rail-Trail follows the valley as it widens, headed south. The creek is also wider and quite placid. The highway is above the trail now as the trail follows the east side of the stream. Travelers pass School House Lane.

The trail hugs some rock ledges and wooden berms as we pedal alongside the creek. Look for fishermen along this section of the trail.

There are DCNR signs throughout this area giving notice of special fishing rules.

They are:

1) Fishing may be done with artificial lure, flies or streamers, natural bait, baitfish, or fishbait. Spinning or fly fishing gear may be used in this area.

2) No trout may be killed or had in possession.

3) Open to fishing year round; there is no closed season.

4) Current trout/salmon permit is required.

I have watched wildlife all through this area and it's always a delight.

A bull frog along the creek.

Common Merganser ducks.

If we are lucky, we may see a Great Blue Heron. These large birds may be seen standing near the water fishing. They are unmistakable because of their size and their prehistoric appearance.

Mile 0.5 (Mile 35.7) Little Slate Run enters Pine Creek from the west. The mountains above Little Slate Run held a narrow gauge railroad that brought logs to the sawmills located on Pine Creek.

An old photo of the trestle at Little Slate Run.

Many old wooden trestles made scenic pictures, but dangerous conditions for the railroad workers.

Mile 1.0 (Mile 36.2) Tomb Flats is one of the newest campgrounds on the Rail-Trail. **Tomb Flats** is one of the **access areas** to the Rail-Trail. It is also a boat access

123

Purple loosestrife and Joe Pye Weed line Pine Creek in August.

point. See page 192 for details and driving instructions.

New restrooms were built in 2015. Camping permits are required here and at all campgrounds along the trail. Check out all the apple trees at this campground.

Looking at the mountains across the creek, we see some of the Tiadaghton State Forest lands. Tiadaghton (pronounced: ty-a-dot-un) was the name the Iroquois gave to Pine Creek, the largest tributary of the West Branch of the Susquehanna River. The exact meaning of the word Tiadaghton is a mystery that may be locked forever in the folklore of the Iroquois Nation. Some think it means "River of Pines".

Most of the land for the Tiadaghton State Forest was purchased between 1900 and 1935 from lumber companies that had removed the

Heading south, Tomb Flats campground is on our right. A comfort station is just off the trail.

The swimming hole at Tomb Flats is quiet today because its raining.

timber and wanted to dispose of the cut-over land. The Civilian Conservation Corps had seven camps within the Tiadaghton State Forest during the 1930's. The Corps constructed and improved the extensive road system and built foot trails and other facilities.

Pennsylvania's 2.2-million-acre state forest system is one the largest certified forests in North America.

There is a local swimming hole in Pine Creek in front of the parking area at Tombs Flats. A large shale ledge flows out into the creek and provides shallow wading before it drops off.

Although there is a picnic table across the stream, there is no easy way to get there. Remember that there are no lifeguards at any casual swimming spot along the trail.

Mile 1.37 (Mile 36.6) Between the Tomb Flats and Black Walnut Bottom Campgrounds, on the right, just off the trail, is an old pioneer cemetery (called the Utceter Cemetery). It is the final resting place for many of the early settlers of the area. Look for the walking stick propped at a tree and the small path through the woods.

This tiny path leads to the pioneer cemetery.

The tombstone for Philip Tomb in this cemetery is not the Pioneer Life author, but a relative.

John Callahan's tombstone is here. He was the son of pioneer settler Dan Callahan. John lived for 100 years. (1791-1891)

All of the tombstones here are from the 1800's.

This is a reverent place where many families, including small children, rest.

Another eagle's nest is in this vicinity. During nesting, between

Tombstones in the pioneer cemetery.

This little bird watched me with curiosity at the cemetery.

April and June usually, the eagle pair regularly flies up and down Pine Creek fishing for food to bring back to the nest. The mountainside rises steeply on the far side of the creek and the Rail-Trail sits high, so eagles often fly past just above eye level. (Pa Game Commission website)

Late spring and early summer are critical times for eaglet development. Please do nothing to disturb the eagles if you see them.

Mile 1.9 (Mile 37.1) Just south of the large island in Pine Creek, we arrive at **Black Walnut Bottom access area**.

It is an access area for both the rail-trail and for watercraft. See page 193 for details and driving instructions.

The Black Walnut Bottom Campground and comfort station lies ahead of us. The delivery entrance for the campground and bathrooms is here at the parking lot. Look for the yellow gate and path on the left side of the parking area.

Black Walnut Campground is a wonderfully serene, shaded, 18 site primitive campground nestled among a stand of trees close to Pine Creek. Callahan Run enters Pine Creek from the west just north of and across from the campground.

The delivery entrance to Black Walnut Bottom campground. It is accessed from the parking area.

The entrance from the rail-trail is a little obtuse. Look for the comfort station sign on the left and the split rail fence on the right.

Among the campsites are large tree stumps that give visitors a sense of some of the logs that were lumbered in this area in the late 1800's and early 1900's. As with all campgrounds along the

The entrance to Black Walnut Bottom Campground from the trail.

rail-trail, a permit is required for overnight camping. There is no running water at the campground.

There are pit toilets. Even if not staying overnight, this is a perfect place to rest. The picnic table tops make comfortable places to stretch out or take a nap.

Black Walnut Bottom Campground is shaded. The comfort station is in the background.

Mile 3.4 (Mile 38.6) We have arrived at the **Clark Farm/Utceter access area.** See page 194 for details and driving instructions.

Trailhead and highway crossing.

Past the yellow gates, the Rail-Trail crosses the highway here. Be careful and cross safely. Although the speed limit is posted, there are many who do not obey the speed limit.

Near the Clark Farm/ Utceter Station access area is the trailhead for one of the finest trails in the area: The Golden Eagle Trail.

Tom Thwaites in his book *50 Hikes of Central Pennsylvania* called the Golden Eagle Trail "the most beautiful day hike in Pennsylvania".

A challenging 10 mile trail, it loops along Bonnell Run, ascends to Raven's Horn, travels the ridgeline until descending along Wolf Run. It has massive vistas, looking north towards Beulahland. It also offers the chance to see the entire Pine Creek Valley and the rail-trail below.

Bonnell Run exits across the highway from the Rail-Trail here. If you have the

(Raven's Horn photo courtesy of Wiki Commons, Nicholas A. Tonelli)

A pretty section of the trail. The highway is just past the split rail fence. Pine Creek is to our right, across the highway. Wolf Run is ahead, on our left.

time and energy, exit the trail and hike just a little of the Golden Eagle trail. The woods are beautiful any time of year.

The next mile headed south is one of the prettiest stretches on the lower section of the Pine Creek Trail. It runs along the east side of the highway as it meanders through the valley. Though the trail is not next to Pine Creek, the fencing between the trail and highway is picturesque.

Mile 3.7 (Mile 38.9) Wolf Run enters below the trail from the east and flows to Pine Creek which is now on our right, traveling south.

There is a sign and small wooden bridge here. Hike just over the berm on the small path to the left and peek at the culvert under the Rail-Trail. A very pretty picture opportunity exists with the bridge above,

Looking back at the trail beyond the creek and culvert at Wolf Run.

the water below, and the lighting through the tunnel.

Be careful here as it is rocky, dark, and footing is tricky.

Mile 4.4 (Mile 39.6) The rail-trail crosses the highway again.

Mile 4.6 (Mile 39.8) The trailhead for the Bob Webber Trail is across the highway at Ross Run. The Bob Webber Hiking Trail is a 1.7 mile out-and-back yellow-blazed path that ascends to the next ridge south of the Golden Eagle Trail.

Bob Webber is a local legend. Webber was a retired forester and was the person primarily responsible for the creation of many hiking trails in this area, including the Golden Eagle Trail, the Black Forest trail, and of course, the Bob Webber trail.

Almost single-handedly, Bob and his ax cleared pathways through the woods over the years.

Bob and his wife Dottie lived off the grid in a log cabin high above Slate Run on the west side of Pine Creek. Once or twice a year Bob hosted a hike on his trails for small groups of fit hikers. Bob died in the spring of 2015.

(Photos of Bob Webber from the Pine Creek Rail-Trail Facebook page)

Mile 4.7 (Mile 39.9) We pass the **Ross Run access area.** (See Page 195 for details and driving instructions)

Mile 5.3 (Mile 40.5) We are approaching the "Golden Spike" location on the 62 mile former railroad bed. On May 9, 1883, engines came together from each direction to meet here. The occasion was the completion of the first railroad through the Pine Creek Valley: the Jersey Shore, Pine Creek, and Buffalo Railroad, also known as the Magee Road.

John Magee was the owner of the railroad until his death. His sons took it over until it was sold eventually to W.H Vanderbilt, known as the Railroad King of America. In September of 1883, Vanderbilt came to inspect the railroad as Col. George Magee's guest. One observation car and two passenger coaches came through here with the locomotive in the rear, so that "the vision of the rail-

way magnates wouldn't be obscured" (Wellsboro Agitator)

A statue with John Magee's bust atop it was erected in December 1886 on the Green in Wellsboro.

Old wooden beams shore up an embankment along the rail-trail.

Mile 5.9 (Mile 41.1) The Rail-Trail cuts through private property on both sides as it heads south to Cammal. Just at the blue "Welcome to Cammal" sign, north of Cammal look across the creek.

The remnants of an old homestead lie there. A local couple lived in this house for years. The way to the house was via a cable car/trolley. The stone "Wishing Well" signaled the path to the house. All of the stones were hauled from Pine Creek by Mr. Wagner and used to build many parts of the house and landscaping. After years, the couple moved to the stone house which they built next to the highway directly across the creek from this site. Both the original homestead and the stone house on the highway have superb stonework. Folks who

The Wishing Well.

grew up in Cammal fondly remember giving the couple a "Honk, hoot, or a holler" to get the cable car sent across the stream for you. The state of Pennsylvania owns the land across the creek now.

When we are across from the stone house across the highway, look at the inscription on the bench on the rail-trail here.

Mile 6.6 (Mile 41.8) Cammal greets us at the completion of this 6.6-mile section of the Pine Creek Rail-Trail. This section has brought us out of the deep recesses of the Pine Creek Gorge and into the vast lumbering valley of yesterday.

(Old photo courtesy of David Ira Kagan, "Pine Creek Villages" Arcadia Publishing)

Perhaps these photos were taken from the same spot, a hundred years between them. These photos both look north, back the way we have come.

CAMMAL TO WATERVILLE

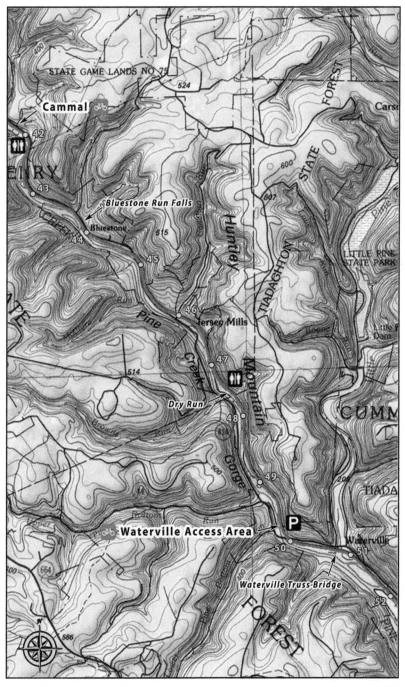

6 CAMMAL TO WATERVILLE

SEGMENT SUMMARY: The Pine Creek Rail-Trail continues its north-south pathway through the Pine Creek Valley past Cammal to Waterville. The Rail-Trail follows the highway closely along a wide, pretty valley until the little town of Jersey Mills. At Jersey Mills, the highway bears right across a modern bridge while the trail continues through an isolated wooded area along Huntley Mountain. There is no access to or exit from the trail once we are on this section of the trail. We exit a mile above Waterville and then follow the back streets of town until we arrive at the Waterville truss railroad bridge and two eating establishments.

This section of the Trail is 8.3 miles.

The mileages in this book are shown in two ways. The first mileage is always the segment mileage; the overall mileage from the Northern Terminus is the second mileage listed.

Mile 0.0 (Mile 41.8) Cammal is a picturesque town with a storied history. Cammal is a contraction of Campbell, the last name of early settlers in the region. Around 1820, Michael Campbell began farming about one mile upstream from Cammal along

Pine Creek. His brothers, Abner and George, built a mill along Mill Run.

During these boom years, the village had stores, four hotels with saloons, four churches, an International Order of Odd Fellows meeting hall (which sometimes doubled as a church), and a weekly newspaper, the Pine Creek Pioneer. Local industries included a hemlock sawmill and other forest-products companies.

In 1905, after the supply of local timber dwindled, the sawmill and other timber-related industries closed. Residents who remained in Cammal found new sources of income: growing and selling ginseng until about 1940 to Chinese buyers from Philadelphia, providing services to tourists and sportsmen, and working for the railroad or the state forestry or highway departments.

Railroad Street parallels the rail-trail and the two are separated by a row of hardwood trees. This makes for a shaded and restful ride through here. There are several beautiful old buildings on this street.

Today, the village still has a few businesses including a restaurant, a campground, and a community center in the former Odd Fellows hall. (Wikipedia, Kagan)

This building, built around 1930 by the Odd Fellow Society served

as a church for 40 plus years. The church was downstairs; the Odd Fellows lodge was upstairs. The basement was used as a social hall. (David Ira Kagan)

Today it is still being used as a branch of the James Brown Library.

This bridge just at the northern edge of the village of Cammal crosses Mill Run, the same Mill Run in the historic photo just below.

Both pictures look north.

(Old photo courtesy of David Ira Kagan, Pine Creek Villages, Arcadia Publishing)

A few blocks to the west, across the stream and near the Lebo Trail, sat the Cammal Civilian Conservation Corp (CCC) Camp (S-124-PA). This camp, like the others in the Pine Creek Valley, ran for a few years in the early to mid 1930's.

The CCC was a post-depression government program meant to put young single men to work on meaningful forest projects. For a more complete description of the CCC program, read pages 40-44 in the Darling Run section of this guidebook)

Be sure to notice the interpretive panels along the Rail-Trail. They can be found at Darling Run, the ghost town of Tiadaghton, Blackwell, Rattlesnake Rock, Slate Run, Cammal, Waterville, Whitetail, and Jersey Shore.

An interpretive panel on the trail.

The panels are housed under a structure that is built to replicate an old train station.

The information on the panels varies from location to location. It includes information about the history of the trail and valley, geology, history of forest fires, Civilian Conservation Corps camps, and town histories. The panels also touch on the influence of the industrial revolution in the area and explore how an environmental restoration of the area began in the 19th and 20th centuries.

According to a Williamsport Sun-Gazette article in 2009, photos and information for the interpretive panels were donated by local residents who also were interviewed about historical tidbits passed down in their family lore.

Mile 0.6 (Mile 42.4) A DCNR "Comfort Station" is located here. Restrooms are spaced along the trail for the convenience of travelers. Some are latrines and some are Comfort stations. The stone-faced buildings with the solar generated turbine vents are Comfort stations. Comfort stations smell somewhat better than latrines.

From here south to mile 44.9, the Trail hugs Pine Creek with the highway a short distance to the east.

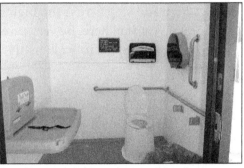

One of the newer bathrooms on the Rail-Trail, Not all of them have baby changing tables.

There are significant gas drilling activities throughout the lower Pine Creek Valley from Truman Run Road, south to Jersey Shore. Frequently, big gas well-related trucks are present on the highways. Special caution should be taken by users of the trail to stay clear of potentially dangerous gas well goings-on. Many roadways and trails in the area have been dis-

The Bluestone Falls just off the highway.

rupted. If you venture off the trail, maps may not accurately portray the land as it exists currently.

Just past Truman Run Road is the little Bluestone Run stream crossing. The name is on the trail bridge. If we hop off our bicycles here and step across the highway, there is a shaded glade and pretty waterfall here. Be very careful on the highway because there is limited place to walk as the guardrails are tight to the highway near the falls.

Mile 2.3 (Mile 44.1) The trail passes the settlement of Bluestone. This town got its name from the blue-gray type of flagstone that was mined in the mountains just east of here.

For those of you who are interested in geocaching, there may be a cache very close to the Trail here. There are several geocaches from here to Jersey Shore on or very near the Rail-Trail.

Mile 3.2 (Mile 45) Past the yellow gates, the rail-trail crosses the highway again. Be careful and cross safely. Although the speed limit is posted, there are many who do not obey the speed limit.

Mile 4.3 (Mile 46.1) We pass through perhaps the tightest set

The view in the Jersey Mills area.

of yellow gates on the entire rail-trail as we cross over Callahan Run. Just south of the bridge was a large water tank for the rail-road. There was also a post office here from 1855 until 2012.

Mile 4.6 (Mile 46.4) The Pine Creek Rail-Trail approaches the village of Jersey Mills. Through this section of the Rail-Trail, the trail parallels State Route 414, with Pine Creek on the far side of the highway. Beyond the bends in the stream, the mountains rise, both to the north and to the south. It is an especially scenic part of the trail.

This old postcard photo was probably taken just south of Jersey Mills.

(Photo courtesy of David Ira Kagan, "Pine Creek Villages", Arcadia Publishing)

141

This photo of flagstone loaded on rail cars is courtesy of David Ira Kagan, "Pine Creek Villages", Arcadia Publishing.

Mile 5 (Mile 46.8) Just south of Jersey Mills, the rail-trail and RT. 414 separate, with the highway crossing to the creek's west side. The Rail-Trail stays on the east side of Pine Creek, as it journeys parallel to the base of Huntley Mountain, elevation 1821 feet. This area is one of the most quietly picturesque.

There is no easy exit from this section of the trail, other than to return to the north to the highway crossing or to continue south to Waterville.

Huntley Mountain is part of a large geological formation that runs throughout mid-Pennsylvania. From here to Waterville, notable rock outcroppings can be observed.

The Huntley Mountain rocks are gray to light olive-gray sandstone with some thin beds of grayish red clay shale. Flagstone has been mined at Huntley Mountain for a century. The railroad was used to move the cut flagstone to market.

David Ira Kagan in his book, "Pine Creek Villages" tells the story of the flagstone boom. There was a large quarry high on the mountain near Callahan Run in the late 1800's. At one time, there were several stone companies in the area.

Flagstone wasn't the only thing transported by the railroad through the years. Early on, coal was the almost exclusive freight, followed by lumber and iron ore. But a variety of fruits from the Lyons, NY area were also transported to cities beyond the railroad line.

Mile 5.9 (Mile 47.7) The Dry Run comfort station is only accessible from the rail-trail. This section of the southern part of the rail-trail is among the most isolated. The highway is far from the trail, across the creek. Homes and camps are across the stream.

Dry Run comfort station.

Opportunities for wildlife viewing abound. Bears have been seen here frequently.

The Pennsylvania Black Bear is one of the smaller bears in North America. They can weigh up to 400 pounds and range in color from black to cinnamon brown. These are powerful, quick animals and have a well-developed sense of smell. Their claws are deadly. Bears eat vegetation, berries, fish, mammals, etc.

Photo courtesy of Bernadette Chiaramonte-Brown, www.theedgeofthewoods.com

In the spring, when cubs are little, mother bears are especially assertive if threatened.

Bears are naturally afraid of humans, but may become "habituated" or accustomed to people along popular hiking trails. Keep

143

the area safe for humans and bears by never feeding or approaching bears.

Should a bear come near you, he is most likely curious or smells something interesting. If he stands up, he is probably not going to attack, but is trying to get a better look or smell. Bear attacks are extremely rare and by comparison a person is about 67 times more likely to be killed by a dog or 90,000 times more likely to be killed in a homicide. (Americanbear.org)

Just remember:

- Stay alert. Be aware of your surroundings.
- Don't surprise a bear. Use caution when traveling in windy weather, down-wind, approaching blind curves, dense vegetation, and noisy streams, where a bear might not see, smell, or hear you coming. Bears will run away, long before you get to them, if they have a chance.
- Circling birds and/or offensive odors may indicate an animal has died and there is a carcass close. Use extra caution in these areas.
- Never leave your food or backpack unattended.

Another elusive animal of local lore is the Pine Creek panther. The panther, or mountain lion, no longer roams the woods of Pennsylvania. According to the Pennsylvania Game Commission, there are no mountain lions in the state. One of the last panthers was killed in Tioga County just before the Civil War in 1862, according to Harry Stevenson, author of "History of the Little Pine Valley."

However, talk continues of hearing piercing shrieks in the night, high in the mountains, the tell-tale call of the panther. The elusive, graceful, big, tawny-colored cat is said by some, to still live in these woods.

Early writers described the characteristic crouch of the panther just before he pounced on his victim for the kill. The panther was said to be up to eleven foot long.

In this area, the panther was called a "painter" Some small towns in Pennsylvania, like Painter Run to the north, are named after the mountain lion. The Penn State University Nittany Lion is a Pennsylvania Panther.

The Nittany Lion statue in State College, PA

On occasion, look up. This wasp nest is directly above the Rail-Trail in this section of

the trail. Wasps nests are a hazard all along the trail, so be safe. Wasps can be in tree nests like this one, in nests built onto yellow gate posts, or even in ground nests.

Mile 7.7 (Mile 49.5) To our west, RT. 414 ends, as it merges with RT. 44. There is a modern bridge across Pine Creek although it is not viewable from the Trail. The Tiadaghton Forest Resource Management district office is on RT. 44, just south of the intersection of the two highways.

We will pass through a tightly forested section of the rail-trail that feels like a tunnel of trees just before we arrive at the Waterville access area. It is dimly lit here in the woods all times of the day.

Mile 8.3 (Mile 50.1) Soon the **Waterville Parking access area** will be in view. There is ample parking here. There are no restrooms. See page 196 for details and driving instructions.

The town of Waterville is about 0.7 mile further to the south.

A rock statue in the middle of Pine Creek. It sports a U.S. Flag.

Cross the highway very carefully here as line-of-sight is limited.

We will parallel a town street to our right as we pedal through a thin woodlot. There are several houses beyond the street that are located along the creek.

We have traveled 8.3 miles on this section of the Trail.

WATERVILLE TO JERSEY SHORE

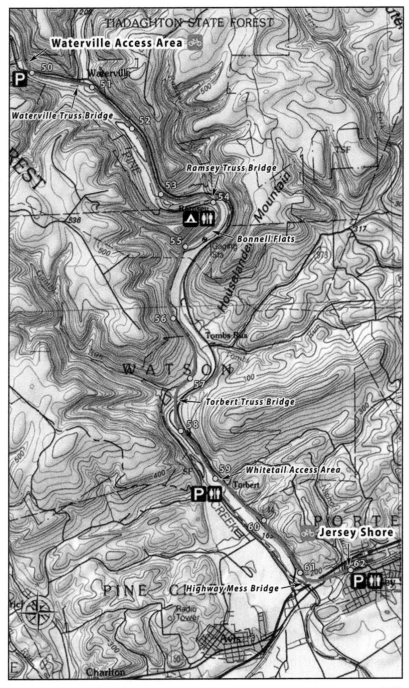

7 WATERVILLE TO JERSEY SHORE

The Pine Creek Rail-Trail continues its north-south pathway through the Pine Creek Valley past Waterville and on to the southern terminus at Jersey Shore. This is the last section of our ride on the rail-trail. It is 11.9 miles long.

SEGMENT SUMMARY: This segment of the trail is the most suburban. We pass the first of three old steel truss bridges in Waterville and then pedal through a long remote section of trail far from the highway, past a small campground, an abandoned Boy Scout camp, and several hiking trails. There will be two more steel truss bridge crossings, a ride along suburban homes and then through farm lands in a wide valley. The trail crosses the highway, and follows along the hillside to an impressive meshed bridge over a four-lane highway. A quick road crossing brings us to the Southern Terminus.

Waterville sits at the confluence of Little Pine Creek and Pine Creek. The First Americans called it the First Fork of the Pine Creek Path, the main Native American trail that was used as the passageway north for a thousand years before the early settlers arrived. There are Three Forks of the Pine Creek Path: the first one is at Waterville, the Second Fork is further north at Blackwell where Babb Creek enters Pine Creek, and the Third Fork is at Ansonia, where Pine Creek meets Marsh Creek.

The Pine Creek Rail-Trail passes all three forks of the Pine Creek Path.

Huntley Mountain rises steeply to a point at the center of the village of Waterville. The mountain and the two streams converging all at one spot make for a geologically busy village.

The mileages in this book are shown in two ways. The first mileage is always the segment mileage; the overall mileage from the Northern Terminus is the second mileage listed.

Mile 0.0 (Mile 50.1) The Waterville access area is almost a mile north of the village of Waterville. After crossing the highway, the trail points itself along a section of houses through a copse of trees.

There are a couple of places to resupply or grab a bite to eat here. McConnell's Country Store is a convenience store well known for their hoagies/subs and soft ice cream. We may also find fly tying equipment, and perhaps even bicycle repair supplies there. And there is the Waterville Tavern next door.

Mile 0.7 (Mile 50.8) Just before the picturesque old railroad bridge, on the highway, is the Waterville Tavern, built in 1825. This building has been in continuous service to the public for the last 190 years or so, at times as a hotel/bunkhouse, a restaurant, and a stagecoach stop.

It's barn has been used as a stable, a dance hall (after the horses were gone) and even a town hall over the years. Stop in for an excellent selection from their menu and bar service. They are family oriented. There are indoor and outdoor tables available.

The Waterville Tavern sits just off the trail in Waterville.

There is a path from the rail-trail into the parking lot that is located between McConnell's Country Store and the Waterville Tavern.

The massive two span Waterville Warren-type through-truss railroad bridge is just before us. This southernmost section of the trail holds three of the four spectacular original steel railroad bridges on the rail-trail.

The Waterville truss bridge on the rail-trail.

Back on the railroad bridge, pause in the middle of it to enjoy the view and to imagine the old steam trains coming through this very location.

Where the concrete highway bridge stands once stood a twin to the quintangular bridge we passed at the north end of Slate Run. There is a sign on the current highway bridge that commemorates the 221-foot Berlin Iron Bridge Company-built bridge that stood here from 1890 until 1984. Its unique look made it an

The lake at Little Pine State Park, taken from the Dam.

architectural beauty. It was removed from here and replaced at Swatara Park in Lebanon County.

About three miles north of here, on Little Pine Creek is Little Pine Dam. The dam was built in 1950 and was one of the first flood control dams in the Susquehanna River Basin. After its erection,

the disastrous floods in the area ceased, except for those caused by Hurricane Agnes in 1972. Little Pine State Park is at the Dam and has a beach, swimming and boating areas, and campgrounds. There is a restaurant near the park.

This old picture is of a splash dam.

In the early logging days, Little Pine Creek played a significant role in the transportation of logs to sawmills built in the Waterville area and further south in Williamsport.

151

This photo is of a log ark.

A splash dam was built on Little Pine Creek above Waterville. The logs would be corralled behind the dam until it was time to release them.

The dam would be opened and the logs would float to their destination.

This was dangerous, but exciting business for the loggers. At times, the logs would jam in the creek. Logs would get snagged on rocks or be stranded on sand bars. Sometimes in these jams, logs would be piled 10 to 15 feet deep for distances upwards to two miles. The log jammer's job was to find the one key log that was holding things back. If they could release that log, the rest would float downstream again.

A flotilla of support workers came along on log drives. Large arks, or house boats, served as dining halls and dorms. Usually, three arks accompanied the drive: a mess hall, a sleeping dorm, and a horse shelter. After every log drive, teams of horses would be deployed to clean up any leftover logs along the way.

The arks would then be disassembled and the wood used up.

Michael and Henry Wolf arrived in the area from Berks County in 1817. They helped to establish Waterville by building a sawmill and clearing some land for farming. A post office was established in Waterville in 1849.

Michael Wolf's daughter Lottie (Lottie Wolf Wheary Wood) was the first person to operate a stagecoach up and down the Little Pine Creek and Big Pine Creek Valley. She carried the mail as well as passengers. In the winter, she changed from driving her stagecoach to using a horse and sleigh when the ground was snow-covered. (Kagan)

Looking east, we catch a view in this 1930's photo of the Waterville railroad bridge and the highway bridge behind it. Pine Creek is in the foreground. Little Pine Creek flows into Pine Creek. The tall mountain to the left is Huntley Mountain Point.

Although the town was laid out by the Wolfs, the first settler in this area was John English, a Revolutionary War veteran.

Just past the last houses in Waterville, there is a large island in the creek. English Island was called Sugar Island originally, named for the sugar maples there. Local legend says that it holds an old cemetery where at least three early settlers were buried by John English.

Mile 1.0 (Mile 51.1) The Rail-Trail and the highway travel close together again until Mile 53. After this, the creek is out of sight to the east.

Photo of the train depot and store at Waterville.

153

A placid part of Pine Creek.

Past the islands, the trail passes a scenic stretch of the creek. It is entirely shaded in this area.

The stone L mileage signs erected by the New York Central Railroad are more regularly seen now. They signify the mileage from the stone sign to Lyons, NY, the railroad's headquarters.

The entire railroad was marked with these one-mile markers. There

were 178 of them. This is old stone marker L-159.

Mile 3 (Mile 53.1) As the Trail and Pine Creek part again, houses start to appear on our right as the trail approaches Ramsey Village. Ramsey Village was settled in 1790 by Thomas Ramsey who was a wagon master for George Washington's Continental Army.

There are a few small road crossings in this area, but there is little traffic here, other than local residents. The trail definitely feels more civilized from this point south.

This old Nelson A. Caulkins postcard looks north and shows the triple span Ramsey Bridge in the foreground. Look closely to see a train on the tracks in the middle of the picture. This is the area we have just pedaled through.

Mile 3.8 (Mile 53.9) The trail bears lazily toward the right, headed south and suddenly the Ramsey steel truss Railroad Bridge appears.

This is the second of the three original railroad bridges we cross on this section of the trail.

Old truss bridges like this were built by the railroads because they were easy to erect in isolated areas, were strong, and economical to build. This three span bridge is absolutely spectacular. Stop on the bridge and soak in the atmosphere.

As we look towards the highway, we will see the old stone walls built by the Works Progress Administration in the 1930's.

This section of the creek is often populated with swimmers. The creek

Photo of the triple span Ramsey bridge courtesy of David Ira Kagan.

here is also high enough to use kayaks and canoes through most of the summer months.

At the Ramsey Bridge, the trail and highway part again.

Towards the east, RT. 44 curves around the bend in the stream. At this point, we will start a large horseshoe shaped crescent. The trail travels the west side of the creek on an almost due easterly direction out to a point at Mile 54. It then swings back almost due westward until Mile 55 when it settles on its usual southern direction. You may not sense this drastic change in direction since Pine Creek is no longer in view for most of the ride here.

This area is called "Beigenbach", German for "Big Bend".

This old postcard shows the large horseshoe curve in the trail just south of here. On the left side of the picture is old Camp Kline, a Boy Scout camp that was active from the 1920's until the 1970's.

Mile 4.5 (Mile 54.6) Bonnell Flats Comfort Station is along the trail here. There is also a water pump. The sign here says we are 7.3 miles from Jersey Shore now.

Here is an opportunity to travel off the trail towards the left, and towards the water. Just past the water pump, headed south, there is a path that heads towards the creek. Follow that to go to the Bonnell Flats campground. This is another campground that can only be accessed from the rail-trail.

The comfort station is on our left. The driveway to the campground is just beyond the comfort station.

Seen from the driveway, the main campground lies ahead. Pine Creek is in the background.

There are also three wooden pavilions that can be used as shelters. Although it's a few hundred feet off the trail, it is a peaceful place to stop and rest.

Overnight camping requires a camping permit from the local DCNR office.

Turk Cap lilies in July.

One of the original Camp Kline buildings is on our left.

There are around 12 campsites here, mostly in the shade.

As we ride south, immediately after the campground, there will be a fence on our left. Just before the

An old postcard showing the Camp Kline suspension bridge.

fence is a small path that takes us directly to the three pavilions in the campground.

Past the fencing on the trail we can see some of the old buildings of Camp Kline.

Imagine this whole area being explored by Boy Scouts and staff over a 50 year period from the 1920's until the 1970's. Of particular note, is the extreme isolation of the camp.

The two ways to access it were by rail or by suspension footbridge. Families would park along RT. 44 and their Scout would walk across the footbridge with backpack in hand.

The wire cable suspension bridge was 25 feet over the water and had a capacity of 14 tons. It was eventually destroyed by tornado-like winds in 1974.

One of the buildings at Camp Kline was unique. The dining hall was originally a dance pavilion in Williamsport. In 1921, it was dismantled, moved here by train, and reassembled. The round dining hall can be seen in this old postcard of Camp Kline.

Just a bit south of here is the trail access point for the Mid State Trail, the same long distance trail we saw a few miles north of Blackwell. Look for a path to our right and an orange blaze on the trees. The trail will almost immediately cross Bonnell Run. The little stream is a great place to wade a little and soak our feet.

The last time I was there, someone had left a sign on the Mid State Trail.

It says 1007.5 all formed with stones.

You may have noticed some really artsy looking white trees along the trail as we have pedaled south. These big trees have distinc-tive bark that flakes off as well as brown- headed round fruit balls that dangle from slim stems even through the winter. These trees can grow to massive size.

An orange blaze marks the Mid- State trail at this little creek crossing.

This is the tree mentioned in the song "Colors of the Wind" from Pocahontas (1995), "How high does a sycamore grow? If you cut it down, then you'll never know."

This adult bald eagle is sitting in a sycamore tree in the fall.

These are sycamore leaves and a fruit ball on the trail in the summer.

Along the Rail-Trail and Pine Creek are many interesting looking plants. Not all of them are welcome here, however.

There are several invasive plants throughout

161

the Pine Creek Valley. Among them are Japanese knotweed, Ailanthus (Tree of Heaven), Mile a Minute, and Japanese Stiltgrass. The PA Department of Conservation and Natural Resources (DCNR) and the Department of Agriculture along with various conservation organizations have joined together to try to prevent the spread of these invasive species.

Invasive plants threaten the natural ecological integrity of the landscape. They compete with native and naturalized plants and often choke out beneficial plants.

Japanese knotweed has a bamboo appearance. It grows rapidly and densely and can easily be seen along the stream banks.

Japanese knotweed

Multiflora rose is a dominant invasive that takes over fields and woodland edges.

Mile a minute was introduced as nursery stock in York County during the 1940's and has become one of the most aggressive and destructive invasive plants in Pennsylvania.

Multiflora rose

It is an annual trailing vine. Its flowers are white and small while the fruits are deep blue and arranged in clusters.

Mile a minute

Japanese Stiltgrass

Japanese Stiltgrass is an annual grass that is native to China, India, Japan, Korea, Malaysia, and the Caucasus Mountains. In 1919, it was introduced in Tennessee, most likely through its use as packing materials. It is found now in several states in the U.S.

The Pennsylvania Department of Conservation and Natural Resources (DCNR) continually works to combat the takeover of areas by these plants. In some cases, the agency considers natural controls, like the use of predator beetles. In other cases, the organization resorts to controlled burning of areas. In the Bonnell Flats area, DCNR conducts controlled burns over 30 acres every other year.

Another concern along the rail-trail is an invasive microscopic algae called Didymo.

There will be signs along the trail imploring visitors to be mindful in not spreading this destructive microorganism. Didymo, also known as "rock snot" smothers stream beds with mats as thick as 8 inches. It is spread by fishing equipment, waders, boats, or anything that comes in contact with it. It can spread to almost any stream.

Visitors are cautioned to disinfect any gear used in Pine Creek or its neighboring streams. We are also asked to clean any recreational equipment that has been in the creek. We are asked to not transport live fish, bait, other critters, plants or water from one body of water to another.

This very serious threat to the pristine stream we are enjoying can only be met and prevented from further spread through conscientious efforts by us all.

A visit to the waterfalls along the fence on the trail.

Mile 5.0 (Mile 55.1) An unnamed tributary south of Bonnell Run comes off the mountain and tumbles along a little waterfall to and under the rail-trail.

There is a fence here that is very picturesque. It's a good place to stop for a bit in the shade and listen to the waterfall. It is fairly easy to step down to the falls. In the early summer, this entire area around the little falls may be full of blossoms.

The water source dries up during dry summers so we may have to be content with a trickle in the falls.

The view under some of the original stone culverts is nice.

Mile 5.4 (Mile 55.5) A natural gas pipeline crosses the Rail-Trail here.

This area was temporarily closed in 2014 while the pipeline was expanded. It has been restored and reseeded. During the pipeline work, several rattlesnakes were taken from this area and relocated.

A view of the mountains and Pine Creek from the pipeline.

Starting in the vicinity of the pipeline, headed south, there is a mile-long island in the creek. As you look across Pine Creek to the east, you are looking at the island and only half of the stream.

We may see some trees down along the trail. In every case, DCNR employees and volunteers work hard to keep the trail in excellent shape for our use.

Fallen trees are cut up and removed almost immediately. Grassy areas are kept mowed and trimmed. In the spring, the rail-trail is swept and prepared for the season.

South of the island, the village of Tombs Run lies across Pine Creek. There will be homes and camps across the water now and on occasion folks may be swimming and enjoying watersports here.

Mile 6.8 (Mile 56.9) The rail-trail turns away from the creek and makes a big bend towards the west.

The Pine Creek Trail comes across this lush valley and past a picturesque farm.

The valley opens up to large cultivated fields and a pristine farm with apple orchards and pastures.

Last year the farmer planted sunflowers. This year the fields are natural.

Mile 7.5 (Mile 57.6) The magnificent three span Torbert steel truss railroad bridge looms. This is the third of the three original bridges located between Waterville and Jersey Shore.

Once you cross the bridge, the highway will be just to the east of the rail-trail again, but Pine Creek will move away from the trail.

The view when southbound from the Torbert bridge.

The rail-trail meanders parallel to and just to the west of Torbert Lane on what feels like the edge of people's yards.

Beautiful homes line the trail. Although there is a feel of village life, the trail is often covered with tree canopy.

Roses and split rail fence mingle.

We ride along fences and suburban buildings.

Mile 8.7 (Mile 58.8) Whenever we catch sight of Pine Creek in this area, we are getting glimpses of the 18 acre Torbert Island Natural Area, just across the stream. About 100 yards away, the island is a "Riparian Forest". The word Riparian is used to describe things growing on, living along, or pertaining to the banks of a natural course of water.

Because there isn't much riparian forest on state forest lands, the island was made a natural area. Sugar maple, river birch, sycamore, and basswood trees can be seen on the island.

Whitetail access area. The parking area is to the left of the drive. The trail access path is straight ahead.

Mile 9.0 (Mile 59.1) The **Whitetail access area** is on the east side of the trail. There is a large parking lot and portable toilets here.

See Page 197 for details and driving instructions.

There is a nice interpretive panel here, just off the parking area.

Mile 10.1 (Mile 60.2) The Rail-Trail crosses the highway again. The Torbert boating access area is just to the west. **This may be one of the more dangerous highway crossings on the rail-trail because of limited visibility.** Please be safe.

The rail-trail hugs the hillsides south of Short Mountain and offers a vast view of farmlands between the highway and Pine Creek which is now far to the west of the trail.

Mile 11 (Mile 61.1) As we head south, RT. 44 turns west just prior to connecting with U.S. RT. 220, a large four lane highway. The Trail passes rock outcrops as it turns east to start the approach to Jersey Shore.

Look carefully and we may see a section of the old original rail lying on the west side of the trail (our right) almost across from old stone marker L-167.

Mile 11.2 (Mile 61.3) Jersey Shore is just ahead. The trail crosses Rt.220 the large, four-lane highway, via a mesh-covered overpass.

Riding through the overhead mesh "tunnel".

We travel on the original railroad bridge that once crossed the highway here.

Mile 11.5 (Mile 61.6) There is a brief uphill pedal here, one of maybe three on the entire trail. Then the Trail crosses Railroad Street in Jersey Shore. Use caution on the highway. This is a spot where traffic may be traveling fast.

Mile 11.9 (Mile 62) Soon the parking area for the Pine Creek Trail's Southern terminus, elevation 655, is in sight.

A large lighted parking lot awaits. There is a Comfort station with flush toilets. There is no drinking water here.

A railroad caboose is on display at the edge of the parking lot. An interpretive panel tells one last story of the trail. And stone marker L-168 sig-nifies that this is the end of the line.

There is an extend-er trail from here that takes us into Jersey Shore for nourishment and town life if you are interested. It adds another mile to our trip.

We have now completed our trip through history via the old original railroad beds that traversed the scenic Pine Creek Valley.

Thanks to all of the folks who created and who maintain this rail-trail for us to enjoy today.

From the marshlands of the far northern section and the deep gorge isolation of the mid sections to the lush fields and massive truss bridges of the southern section, it has been magical. Thanks for coming with me.

THE BRIDGES OF THE PINE CREEK RAIL TRAIL

MILE	BRIDGE DESCRIPTION
4.3	The Lower Marsh Creek Modern Arch bridge
24.6	The Blackwell plate girder bridge over Pine Creek
29.1	The three span Truss bridge at Cedar Run
50.8	The two span Truss bridge at Waterville
53.9	The three span Truss bridge at Ramsey
57.6	The three span Truss bridge at Torbert
61.3	The Overhead Mesh bridge at RT. 220

TRIP PLANNING   8

So, you are thinking of biking all or part of the Pine Creek Rail-Trail. This trail is a favorite for easy, level, long-distance bike touring through a variety of natural environments. From the wetlands and farms of the north, to the isolated, rugged, canyons of Pine Creek, and ultimately to the wide, historic valley as we cruise into the southern terminus, this ride will reward takers with relaxed, picturesque, hours of pedaling.

The following sections of the guidebook answer questions and guide you through some decisions in order to make the trip as enjoyable and safe as possible.

9

WHAT DO YOU WANT TO KNOW

HOW LONG IS THE TRAIL?

The trail distance from the Northern Terminus, three miles north of Wellsboro, PA to the Southern Terminus on Railroad Street in Jersey Shore, PA is about 62 miles.

WHAT IS THE TRAIL LIKE?

The Pine Creek Rail-Trail is paved with firmly packed, compacted limestone. It generally has a smooth and even riding surface.

The trail, since it is built on a railroad bed is fairly level. The grade along the entire trail is about 2% downhill from Wellsboro to Jersey Shore. The grade difference is barely noticeable. Some riders say it equates to about a one gear difference in riding gear, heading north.

Headwinds determine the choice of bike gear more than grade, though.

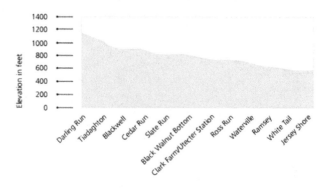

The Path width is about 8 foot across at its narrowest. The edges of the trail may not be as compacted so there may be loose gravel there. In places, the trail is split between one side used for hiking/biking and the other side which is exclusive for horses.

WHAT BIKE IS BEST TO USE?

Most folks use a hybrid or mountain bike on the rail-trail. Both work fine, since the tires are larger and slightly knobby. Some people ride recumbent bikes or trikes on the trail.

WHERE DO I SLEEP? WHERE WILL I EAT?

There is plenty of lodging in the towns at either terminus. There are camp rentals along the trail also. Of note is the Hotel Manor in Slate Run and the Cedar Run Inn and Pettecoat Junction campground in Cedar Run. Cedar Run is about at the half-way mark on the trail.

Primitive campgrounds are right on the trail. They require camping permits. The permits are free, but require contact with either the Tioga State Forest or Tiadaghton State Forest district office.

Towns along the way have grocery stores, convenience stores, and restaurants.

In Wellsboro, near the northern terminus, there are many excellent food establishments, ranging from fast food and convenience stores to fine dining. Right at the Northern Terminus, Pag-Omar Farms is a family owned convenience store and farm market.

There are no towns though, between the Northern Terminus and Blackwell, a stretch of 25 miles and, therefore, there is no reliable or easy opportunity for food or drink resupply.

In Blackwell, there is a general store. Another 5 miles south is the town of Cedar Run where there is a fine dining restaurant (with limited hours) and inn as well as a general store. Both are usually open during the day on weekends. The Cedar Run store is open mostly in the afternoons, but closes for the winter months.

Five miles south of Cedar Run, the town of Slate Run has Wolfe's General Store and the Hotel Manor, a full dining restaurant and hotel near the trail.

In Waterville, 16 miles further south, there is McConnell's Country store and the Waterville Tavern.

At Jersey Shore, near the Southern Terminus there are many and varied food establishments.

There are no reliable water sources on many sections of the Trail. Carrying ample water supply is recommended.

IS IT DANGEROUS?

This is a long-distance recreational trail with natural hazards— weather, wildlife, and temporary trail conditions.

It is important to be alert as you ride along. And equally, it is important to be well prepared. Knowledge of the area, weather, your own limitations, and some common sense will help.

It is always wise to travel with others on any trail. There will be other riders you will meet along the way, so you will probably never be alone for long. There has not been any trail violence to date, but being alert and self-protective is wise. Remember that some long sections of the Trail are very remote with no easy access or exit. In case of emergency, response times could be prolonged by the terrain. And dusk comes early in the deep gorge section of the rail-trail.

There is no reliable cell service along almost the entire trail.

According to a cell phone guide published by the Pine Creek Shuttle Service:

"Neither cell phone or texting service is available in the valley from Wellsboro Junction to Slate Run. Cell phone and texting are usually available at Wolfe's store in Slate Run, and McConnell's store in Waterville, as well as the Happy Acres store (north of) near Waterville. Texting is sometimes available in Cammal. From

Ramsey down, there generally is both cell phone and texting service. (The above information was tested with Verizon and could change with other providers and upgraded cell towers)."

WHAT DO I NEED TO TAKE WITH ME?

An absolute is plenty of water. It is imperative that you stay hydrated. There are a few water pumps along the trail, but even if they are working, the water has a strong metallic taste. Since water is not reliably available, bring plenty of your own.

It is also good to take snacks, jerky, energy bars, or other quick nourishments that are easily packable.

Packing a simple bike repair kit is also encouraged. A spare tube, some tire levers, a tube patch kit, and a mini air pump will suffice. Bring directions along if you don't know how to change your bike tire.

A first aid kit, sunscreen, and very importantly, insect repellent are necessary.

Pennsylvania and New York lead the country in the number of tick bites. It is important that you properly protect yourself from ticks in all rural areas.

Extra clothes in case of a downpour or a change of weather are handy. Binoculars can be helpful, and of course, by all means, bring your camera!

WHAT IS A "COMFORT STATION"?

Comfort stations, also known simply as pit toilets, are available at intervals along the trail. Some are simple latrines; others are fancier with solar powered vents, skylights, baby changing stations, and hand sanitizer.

COMFORT STATIONS ALONG THE TRAIL

MILE	LOCATION	MILE	LOCATION
4.8	Marsh Creek	32.5	Hilborn Fields
8.7	Darling Run	36.2	Tomb Flats
11.8	Turkey Path	37.1	Black Walnut Bottom
16.1	Tiadaghton	42.4	Cammal
24.5	Blackwell	47.7	Dry Run
25.3	Hoffman Campground	54.6	Bonnell Flats
26.4	Rattlesnake Rock	59.1	Whitetail
		62	Jersey Shore

CAN I RENT A BIKE THERE OR HAVE MY CAR SHUTTLED FOR ME?

Yes, Pine Creek Outfitters is a stellar business not far off the rail-trail in Ansonia towards the northern end of the trail. They rent bicycles. They also do shuttle service, whether you have your own bike or not. They can pick you up or drop you off at several locations along the trail.

Wolfe's general store in Slate Run and Bonner Sports and RV on RT. 44 north of Jersey Shore rent bikes, also.

Pine Creek Shuttle Service does shuttles also. They are located closer to the southern end of the trail.

All of these businesses have web pages and can be easily searched on the internet.

DO I HAVE TO DO THE WHOLE TRAIL AT ONCE?

No. The trail conveniently has access and parking areas every 7 or 8 miles, for the most part. This book's sections highlight seven easy-to- ride segments. An out-and-back ride to the same access point will take probably three hours, at a leisurely pace.

PINE CREEK RAIL TRAIL PRIMITIVE CAMPGROUNDS

MILE	DESCRIPTION
16.1	Tiadaghton
25.2	Hoffman Campground
36.2	Tomb Flats
37.1	Black Walnut Bottom
54.6	Bonnell Flats

10 RULES AND REGULATIONS
DCNR Published Rules

HOURS OF USE

The trail is open to the public from one-half hour before sunrise until one-half hour after sunset. Overnight parking in designated areas is limited to those with a valid camping permit.

General trail use is a daytime activity. Using the trail and parking areas after dark for legitimate activities, such as night fishing, night hikes, or night skiing in winter is allowed. However, unauthorized trail use is not allowed, a rule which is aggressively enforced.

HELMETS

State law requires all bike riders and passengers under the age of 12 to wear a helmet.

EMERGENCIES

Contact Lycoming or Tioga County Communication Center by dialing 911.

PRIVATE LANDS

Trail users must respect the rights and privacy of adjoining private property owners. Please do not leave the trail or right–of–way through private property, except at clearly designated and marked exit and entry points.

ROAD CROSSINGS

Trail users must come to a complete stop and look both ways at all public road crossings. The trail is gated and signed at all such crossings. Private crossings may be gated, and are signed with stop or yield signs as appropriate.

HORSES AND DOGS

Horseback riding and horse-drawn vehicles are permitted on the service road adjacent to the improved trail, from Ansonia south to Tiadaghton. They are only permitted to utilize the improved trail designated for bicycles and skiers when crossing bridges.

Unleashed dogs are not permitted on the trail right-of-way, in the parking areas, or campgrounds. Leashes must not exceed six feet in length.

BRIDGES

Fishing, jumping, or diving from, or climbing onto trail bridges is not permitted.

ALCOHOL

Consumption of alcoholic beverages on the trail right-of-way is prohibited. Intoxication while operating a bicycle is a crime, as is public drunkenness in parking areas and camping areas, along the trail right-of-way, as well as on the trail right-of-way itself. These regulations will be vigorously enforced.

FIREARMS

Firearms shall not be loaded while on the trail right-of-way, parking lots, or campgrounds, except between Blackwell and Wellsboro Junction where use of the trail for hunting is at the sole discretion of the district forester. It is recommended that trail users wear fluorescent orange (hunter orange) during the fall hunting season for personal safety.

SPECIAL COMMERCIAL

Special organized group or commercial use activity on the trail or trail right-of-way requires a Special Activity Agreement or Letter of Authorization with the Department.

CAMPING

All camping along Pine Creek requires a camping permit. All camping must take place at least 100 feet from waterways. Camping on the right-of-way or in trail parking lots is not permitted. Groups of more than 10 people must obtain a Letter of Authorization from the district forester in addition to a camping permit.

Tiadaghton State Forest: Primitive camping near the rail-trail is permitted at Black Walnut Bottom Camping Area (2 miles south of Slate Run). Black Walnut Bottom offers picnic tables, fire rings, and restrooms. Canoeists with permits may also camp at a limited number of sites at Naval Run, Callahan Run, and at Bonnell Flats Camping Area. Permits are available at the district office, and can be issued in person, by US mail, or by fax. (Camping is also permitted at Tombs Flats now.)

Tioga State Forest: Primitive camping near the rail-trail is permitted along Pine Creek at designated locations. Tiadaghton and Hoffman Campgrounds offer picnic tables, fire rings, potable water, and restrooms. Permits are available at the district office, and can be issued in person, by US mail, or by fax.

DISTANCE IN MILES

Northern Terminus at Stokesdale To Ansonia 7.3

Ansonia to Darling Run 1.4

Darling Run to Tiadaghton 7.4

Tiadaghton to Blackwell 8.5

Blackwell to Rattlesnake Rock 1.8

Rattlesnake Rock to Cedar Run Bridge 2.7

Cedar Run Bridge to Hilborn Fields 3.4

Hilborn Fields to Slate Run 2.7

Slate Run to Black Walnut Bottom 1.9

Black Walnut Bottom to Ross Run 2.8

Ross Run to Cammal 1.9

Cammal to Dry Run 5.9

Dry Run to Waterville 2.4

Waterville to Bonnell Flats 4.5

Bonnell Flats to Torbert 3.0

Torbert to Jersey Shore 4.4

Northern Terminus to Southern Terminus 62.0

12 THE RAIL-TRAIL IN WINTER

Winter activities are available on the Rail-Trail. It is groomed by the Pennsylvania Department of Conservation and Natural Resources (DCNR) for cross country skiing. The trail is also used for hiking and snowshoeing.

The bridge on the northern section of the trail is beautiful all times of the year, but it takes on a special beauty in the winter.

*(Picture courtesy of Bernadette Chiaramonte-Brown,
www.theedgeofthewoods.com)*

Winter brings a different perspective to the trail. After a snow-fall, the trail is even more magical than it ever is.

As always, the trail brings visitors to spectacular and remote scenery. Use caution in cold weather to protect from exposure. Again, emergency response times by the nature of the remoteness of the trail are extended during the snowy and icy winter months.

A word about when winter comes, here in northern Pennsylvania. Usually, the first snowflakes fall in early November. But, there have been massive snowfalls in October on occasion. The hard winter months are January and February. There is often one last snowstorm in March. At lower elevations and in town, the trail calls to us in March but it is not safe then. Most hiking trails reopen in mid-April. The earliest I ride is mid-April, and even then, there is snow along the trail. Be safe.

WEATHER INFORMATION BY MONTH

MONTH	AVG HIGH TEMP (°F)	AVG LOW TEMP (°F)	AVG PRECIP-ITATION (INCHES)	SUNRISE AM	SUNSET PM
Jan	33.1	15.3	13.3	7:27	5:17
Feb	36.1	16.0	10.3	7:05	5:42
Mar	44.8	22.9	12.1	7:21	7:15
Apr	58.1	33.4	13.8	6:30	7:50
May	68.6	43.3	13.2	5:50	8:22
Jun	77.0	53.7	13.1	5:34	8:46
Jul	81.4	58.1	12.5	5:48	8:42
Aug	79.2	56.6	10.8	6:17	8:09
Sep	71.2	49.2	11.1	6:49	7:19
Oct	59.9	37.8	12.2	7:21	6:28
Nov	47.7	30.8	13.1	6:58	4:49
Dec	36.5	20.6	12.3	7:29	4:39

In every walk with nature, one recieves far more than he seeks - John Muir

TRAIL ACCESS AREAS 13

There are several access areas for the Pine Creek Rail-Trail. Some have more amenities than others. All of them have parking near the rail-trail. Most have these blue signs letting visitors know the mileage along the rail-trail at nearby locations.

All access points can be accessed easily by highway. Some are poorly marked, however. GPS driving coordinates are listed in the Guidebook, if no street address is available.

From North to South, the trail access areas are listed on the next pages. There are additional access points for boating purposes.

NORTHERN TERMINUS/BUTLER ROAD (Stokesdale)

The Butler Road access area has:

- A medium sized dirt parking lot
- Porta-johns
- Trail maps at the information board
- Cell phone service

(Directions are listed in the "Finding the Northern and Southern Terminus" Section of the Book on Page 199)

MARSH CREEK (Ansonia)

The Ansonia access area has:

- A dirt parking lot.
- There are no restrooms or amenities here.
- Wagon rides enter and exit here.
- One side of the trail from this point south to Tiadaghton is designated for horse traffic.

Directions From Wellsboro: Driving coordinates: 1452 Marsh Creek Rd, Wellsboro, PA. Take RT. 660/362 West for 9 miles to RT. 6. Turn left onto Route 6 West. Immediately past the RT. 6 bridge, turn right onto RT. 3027 (Marsh Creek Rd). Travel .4 miles to the parking area on the right.

DARLING RUN

The Darling Run access area has:

- Large parking areas
- Restrooms
- Water
- Land phone for local calls
- Interpretive panel
- Handicap accessibility
- **NO CELL PHONE SERVICE**

Directions From Wellsboro: Driving coordinates: near 2936 Colton Rd, Wellsboro, PA. Take RT. 660/362 west from Wellsboro for 8.3 miles. Turn sharply left on a backwards turn downhill at the wooden Access Area sign. Travel .4 miles into parking area.

GPS coordinates: 41.736915, -77.428651

BLACKWELL

The Robert McCollough, Jr. parking area is intended to be a watersports parking area. Bicyclists are expected to park 1.8 miles south of here at Rattlesnake Rock. This parking area has:

- Handicap accessibility
- Restrooms and water
- Land Phone for local calls
- Interpretive panel
- Boating Access
- **NO CELL PHONE SERVICE**

Directions From Wellsboro: Driving coordinates: Near 955PA. RT. 414, Morris, PA. Take RT. 287 11.7 miles to Morris, PA. Turn onto RT. 414, West for 5.3 miles. Travel past the general Store and the rail-trail and into the parking area on the left at the wooden Access Area sign.

GPS Coordinates: 41.556393, -77.381535

RATTLESNAKE ROCK

This is the official bicycle access point for the Rail-Trail. This access area has:

- Restrooms
- Handicap accessibility
- Land phone for local calls
- Interpretive Panel
- **NO CELL PHONE SERVICE**

Directions From Wellsboro: Driving coordinates: 21874 RT. 414, Morris, PA. Take RT. 287 11.7 miles to Morris, PA. Turn onto RT. 414, West for 5.3 miles to the bridge over Pine Creek. Continue on RT. 414 for another 1.8 miles to the parking area on left. A large wooden sign marks the area.

GPS Coordinates: 41.540745, -77.405358

SLATE RUN

The Slate Run parking access area is next to Pine Creek west of the trail and the highway. It has:

- Handicap accessibility
- Large Parking area
- Boating access
- Nearby restaurant and general store
- ATM inside general store
- Nearby wireless Internet and cell service
- **NO CELL SERVICE ON THE TRAIL OR IN THE LOT**
- Interpretive panel

Directions From Wellsboro: Take RT. 287 South 11.7 miles to Morris, PA. Turn onto RT. 414, West for 16 miles to Slate Run. Just south of Wolfe's General Store, turn right onto Slate Run Road. The bridge over Pine Creek is on Slate Run Rd. The Parking area is on the right, before the bridge.

Directions From Jersey Shore: From RT. 220 near Jersey Shore, PA, turn north onto RT. 44. Follow RT. 44 North/ RT. 414 East for 27.3 miles to Slate Run. Stay on RT. 414, north of Waterville. Just south of Wolfe's General Store, turn left onto Slate Run Road. The bridge over Pine Creek is on Slate Run Rd. The Parking area is on the right, before the bridge.

The address at Wolfe's General Store is 14167 PA RT. 414, Slate Run, PA.

GPS Coordinates for the parking area: 41.471070, -77.501895

TOMB FLATS

Although this is an unmarked and unofficial access area, Tomb Flats allows access to the rail-trail via the campground parking lots. It is reached via Pa Route 44/414, one mile south of Slate Run. There is a tiny dirt driveway to get to the parking lots. The parking area is between the highway and Pine Creek. You will cross the Rail-Trail to park. Tomb Flats has:

- A medium sized parking lot
- Camping area
- Boating access
- Handicap accessibility
- **NO CELL PHONE SERVICE**

Directions From Wellsboro: Take RT. 287 South 11.7 miles to Morris, PA. Turn onto RT. 414, West for 16 miles to Slate Run. The unmarked turnoff is one mile south of Wolf's General Store. The Parking area is on the right. The driving coordinates are close to Yoder Lane, Slate Run.

Directions From Jersey Shore: From RT. 220 near Jersey Shore, PA, turn north onto RT. 44. Follow RT.44 North/RT. 414 East for 26.2 miles. Stay on RT. 414 north of Waterville. The unmarked parking area is on the left. The driving coordinates are close to Yoder Lane, Slate Run.

GPS coordinates: 41.457315, -77.509949

BLACK WALNUT BOTTOM

Black Walnut Bottom access area is reached via PA Route 44/414, 1.8 miles south of Slate Run. The parking area is between the highway and Pine Creek. You will cross the Rail-Trail to park. Black Walnut Bottom has:

- A small parking lot
- Camping area
- Boating access
- Handicap accessibility
- **NO CELL PHONE SERVICE**

Directions From Wellsboro: Take RT. 287 South 11.7 miles to Morris, PA. Turn onto RT. 414, West for 16 miles to Slate Run. The poorly marked turnoff is 1.8 miles south of Wolf's General Store. The Parking area is on the right. The driving coordinates are close to 11800 PA RT. 414, Cammal, PA.

Directions From Jersey Shore: From RT. 220 near Jersey Shore, PA, turn north onto RT. 44. Follow RT.44 North/RT. 414 East for 25.4 miles. Stay on RT. 414 north of Waterville. The poorly marked parking area is on the left. The driving coordinates are close to 11800 PA RT. 414, Cammal, PA.

GPS coordinates: 41.447765, -77.517396

CLARK FARM/UTCETER STATION

The Clark Farm Utceter Station access area is a small pull off area near Bonnell Run and the trailhead to the Golden Eagle Trail. The access area has:

- Comfort station
- Gravel parking area
- Camping
- Boating access
- **NO CELL PHONE SERVICE**

Directions From Wellsboro: Take RT. 287 South 11.7 miles to Morris, PA. Turn onto RT. 414, West for 18.6 miles to the parking area. Parking is on the right, near Pine Creek.

Directions From Jersey Shore: From RT. 220 near Jersey Shore, PA, turn north onto RT. 44.Follow RT. 44North/ RT. 414 East for 24.7 miles. Stay on RT. 414 north of Waterville. The parking area is on the left near the creek.

GPS Coordinates: 41.439139, -77.510559

Ross Run has a small parking and access area. It is near the trail head of the Bob Webber Trail and Wolf Run Bald vista. The area is clearly marked. The parking area has:

- Handicap Accessibility
- Boating access
- Small gravel parking lot
- **NO CELL PHONE SERVICE**

Directions From Wellsboro: Take RT. 287 South 11.7 miles to Morris, PA. Turn onto RT. 414, West for 20.3 miles to the parking area. Parking is on the right, near Pine Creek.

Directions From Jersey Shore: From RT. 220 near Jersey Shore, PA, turn north onto RT. 44.Follow RT. 44 North/ RT. 414East for 23 miles. Stay on RT. 414 north of Waterville. The parking area is on the left near the creek.

GPS Coordinates: 41.420650, -77.488205

The Waterville Access Area is .7 miles north of the village of Waterville on RT. 44/414. It has:

- Gravel parking area
- Handicap Accessibility
- Interpretive panel
- **NO CELL PHONE SERVICE**
- No restrooms

Waterville Access Area	
Dry Run Comfort Station	2.5 Mi. →
Cammal Comfort Station	7.9 Mi. →
Bonnell Flat Comfort Station & Campground (Permits Required)	4.3 Mi. ←
Whitetail Access Area	8.8 Mi. ←

Directions From Wellsboro:
Take RT. 287 South 11.7 miles to Morris, PA. Turn onto RT. 414, West for 28.7 miles to the parking area. Parking is on the left, immediately after crossing Pine Creek on the highway bridge.

Directions From Jersey Shore: From RT. 220 near Jersey Shore, PA, turn north onto RT. 44.Follow RT. 44 North/RT. 414 East for 14.6 miles. The parking area is on the right immediately before crossing Pine Creek on the highway bridge.

GPS Coordinates: 41.311375, -77.376693

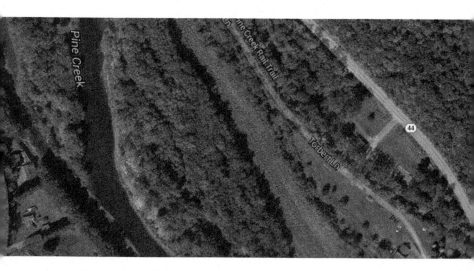

The Whitetail parking area is a large gravel lot that looks like it is part of someone's residence area. It has:

- Handicap Accessibility
- **CELL PHONE SERVICE**
- Interpretive panel
- Portable toilets

Directions From Jersey Shore: Driving Coordinates: 1749 PA 44, Jersey Shore, PA. From the intersection of Tiadaghton Ave and RT. 220 near Jersey Shore, turn north onto RT. 44. Follow RT. 44 North/RT. 414 East for 1.8 miles. The parking area is on the left.

GPS Coordinates: 41.216750, -77.313931

SOUTHERN TERMINUS/ JERSEY SHORE

The Jersey Shore access parking lot is on Railroad Street in Jersey Shore. It is a nicely lit, large parking area with comfortable restrooms. It has:

- Handicap accessibility
- Restrooms
- Interpretive panel
- RV/Bus turnaround
- **CELL PHONE SERVICE**

(Directions are listed in the "Finding the Northern and Southern Terminus" Section of the Book on Page 200)

FINDING THE NORTHERN AND SOUTHERN TERMINUS 14

FINDING THE NORTHERN TERMINUS (MILE 0.0)

From Wellsboro: Driving Coordinates: near 222 Butler Rd, Wellsboro, PA. Take RT. 6 West/RT. 287 North from town. Travel 2.7 miles and continue onto RT. 287 North. Travel 0 .6 mile to Butler Rd. Turn left onto Butler Rd. Drive to the intersection and make a left towards Pag-Omar Farms. Drive past Pag-Omar Farms and into the parking lot of the Northern Terminus. The Rail-Trail starts at the end of the lot.

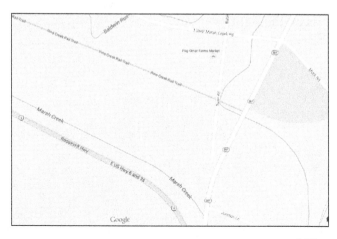

199

FINDING THE SOUTHERN TERMINUS (MILE 62)

Driving Coordinates: near 515 Railroad St, Jersey Shore, PA.

Driving south on RT. 220: take the Thomas Street Exit. Go over the highway and go .1 mile on Thomas Street to High Street. Take a right onto High St. Drive three blocks and turn left onto Meadow Alley Drive two blocks to Railroad Street. Turn right and drive .1 mile. Parking lot is on the left.

Driving north on RT. 220: take the RT. 44 Exit. Follow the exit to RT. 44 (Tiadaghton Street). Turn right. Turn left onto East Central Ave/ Woodard Ave. Follow East Central Ave/Woodard Ave for .3 mile. Just after the bridge across Pine Creek, the street becomes Railroad St. Follow Railroad St. for .7 mile. Parking lot is on the right.

EPILOGUE

At the Southern Terminus, the Pine Creek Rail-Trail finishes its 62-mile journey. The landscape has changed in typology from the early wetland miles along the Northern Terminus section and the deep isolation of the Pine Creek Gorge with its steep canyon-like walls, to the wide valley pedal path along the highway and through the small hamlets of the south.

But the path traveled on the Rail-Trail is essentially the same path that was traveled by the First Nation citizens along the Pine Creek Path and by the steam and diesel locomotives that brought freight, lumber, and coal through the exact same locations.

In the 21st century, the trail stays true to its beginnings over hundreds, even thousands of years.

Time brings different residents and visitors, but the land is the same. Pristine beauty provides the perfect backdrop for careful adventure along a well-maintained, well-kept multipurpose trail.

Be safe. Don't damage this beautiful asset. And may Pine Creek and the surrounding areas survive through the stewardship of all of us.

Look deep into nature and then you will understand everything better - Albert Einstein

CITATIONS

1. "51 Great Places to Hike". USA Today. Gannett. Retrieved June 25, 2011.

2. Biking the Pine Creek Rail Trail. Pine Creek Outfitters. Retrieved Jan 10, 2015

3. Bly, Laura (July 27, 2001). "10 great places to take a bike tour". USA Today. p. 3D.

4. Campbell, A. Wayne. "Recollections of the Fall Brook Railroad" Self-Published 1998

5. Claudius Boatman: Separating the Man from the Myth. WordPress.com Retrieved Jan 30, 2015

6. Dillon, Chuck. "Explore: Pennsylvania's Grand Canyon: Short Hikes in the Tioga State Forest", Wellsboro: Pine Creek Press. 1992

7. Dillon, Chuck. "Pennsylvania Grand Canyon, a Natural and Human History", Wellsboro: Pine Creek Press, 2006

8. Fergus, Charles (2002). "Natural Pennsylvania: Exploring State Forest Natural Areas": Mechanicsburg, Pennsylvania: Stackpole Books. pp. 189–193. ISBN 0-8117-2038-1.

9. Glimm, James York. "Flatlanders and Ridgerunners: Folktales from the Mountains of Northern Pennsylvania". New York: University of Pittsburgh Press, 1983

10. Kagan, David Ira. "Pine Creek Villages" Charleston, SC: Arcadia Publishing. 2008

11. Kraybill, Spencer L. Pennsylvania's Pine Creek Valley and Pioneer Families. Gateway Publishing: 1991

12. McGlade, William G. "Pennsylvania Trail of Geology, Leonard Harrison and Colton Point State Parks, The Grand Canyon of Pennsylvania, Geologic Features of Interest (Park Guide 5)" (PDF). Pennsylvania Department of Conservation and Natural Resources. Retrieved 2013-07-01.

13. Meginness, John F. "History of Lycoming County, Pennsylvania. Chicago: Brown, Rink, and Company, 1892

14. Meagher, John. History of Tioga County, Pennsylvania. Chicago: R.C. Brown and Company, 1897

15. "National Natural Landmark: Pine Creek Gorge". National Park Service. Retrieved September 30, 2008.

16. Nessmuk (Sears, George Washington) Woodcraft and Camping: New York: Doves Publishers (1854)

17. Nessmuk (Sears, George Washington) Forest Runes.: New York: Field and Stream Publishing (1887)

18. Owlett, Steven E. Seasons Along The Tiadaghton: An Environmental History of the Pine Creek Gorge (1st Edition ed.). Petaluma, California: Interprint. ISBN 0-9635905-0-2. (1993).

19. Pennsylvania Department of Conservation and Natural Resources, Bureau of Forestry (Oct 2012). Pine Creek Rail Trail (Map). 1 1/4 inch is 1 mile. Retrieved March 9, 2015.

20. Pennsylvania Department of Conservation and Natural Resources, Bureau of Forestry (May 2008). West Rim Trail (Map). 2 ½ inch is 1 mile. Retrieved on March 9, 2015.

21. Pennsylvania Department of Conservation and Natural Resources, Bureau of Forestry (May 2011). Tioga State Forest (Map). 1 inch is 2 miles. Retrieved on March 9, 2015.

22. "Pine Creek Gorge". Pennsylvania Department of Conservation and Natural Resources. Retrieved September 30, 2008.

23. Pine Creek Path, Wikipedia, Retrieved Aug. 21, 2015

24. Pine Creek Watershed. Biological Resources. Retrieved Jan 10, 2015

25. "Rail-Trails Pennsylvania, New Jersey, and New York" Birmingham, Al: Wilderness Press. 2011

26. Rails to Trails Conservancy, Poll, Top Ten Trails in PA, posted 9/30/2014.

27. Stoving, Richard L. "Wellsboro's Own Railroad" Hanover Pa: The Railroad Press. 2003

28. Stephenson, Harry, "History of Little Pine Valley" Camp Hill, 1992

29. Susquehannock Trail Club. STC Newsletter: Capturing a Wild Elk. Retrieved on March 8, 2015

30. Tioga County Historical Society Bicentennial Committee, "Tioga County PA: The First Two Hundred Years". The Donning Company Publishers, 2004

31. The CCC Years. History of the Pennsylvania State Parks. Pennsylvania Department of Conservation and Natural Resources. Retrieved on Jan 6, 2015.

32. The Pennsylvania Lumber Museum - History. Pennsylvania Historical and Museum Commission. Retrieved Feb 1, 2015.

33. The Pine Creek Rail Trail. Pinecreekvalley.com Retrieved Jan 26, 2015

34. Tome, Philip. "Pioneer Life or Thirty Years a Hunter". Harrisburg, Pa: Aurand Press, 1928

35. Wallace, Paul A.W. "Indian Paths of Pennsylvania" Harrisburg, PA Pennsylvania State Historical and Museum Commission, 1961

ABOUT THE AUTHOR

In 2013, Linda Stager retired from a 40-year career in human services administration. After that, she re-learned how to ride a bicycle and adapted hers for day-long jaunts, replete with panniers and wicker basket.

Early on, Linda set out looking for flat, easy terrain for riding. A resident of Wellsboro, Linda soon found the Pine Creek Trail, just a few miles from her house. She learned how to strap her bike on the back of her car and she was soon spending quality time on the Trail.

A licensed social worker by trade, Linda enjoys quiet listening. She was struck by the soft sounds of the Pine Creek Trail. She set out to document her trips, with photos, and by learning all she could about its rich history.

Linda sometimes uses a Panasonic Lumix point and shoot for her "go-to" trekking camera, but usually she can be seen on the trail with her Nikon DSLR with its 150-600 mm lens.

She always enjoys the Rail-Trail, even in the rain.

It's the way you ride the trail that counts. - Dale Evans

CPSIA information can be obtained at www.ICGtesting.com
Printed in the USA
BVOW07s0821270216

438125BV00002BA/3/P